Italic Handwriting for Young People

by Fred Eager

COLLIER BOOKS
A Division of Macmillan Publishing Co., Inc.
NEW YORK

COLLIER MACMILLAN PUBLISHERS
LONDON

PERMISSIONS

Page 60: "Riddle: What am I?" by Dorothy Aldis, reprinted by permission of G. P. Putnam's Sons from *Hop, Skip and Jump* by Dorothy Aldis. Copyright 1934 by Dorothy Aldis; renewed.

Page 72: "Bundles" by John Farrar, reprinted by permission of Yale University Press from *Songs for Parents* by John Farrar, Copyright 1921.

Page 74: "Dreidel Song" by Ephraim Rosenzweig from *Now We Begin* by Marian J. and Ephraim M. Rosenzweig. Copyright 1937 by The Union of American Hebrew Congregations. Reprinted by permission of the publisher.

Page 88: Excerpted from *Nadita* by Grace Moon. Copyright 1927 by Doubleday and Co., Inc. Reprinted by permission of the publisher.

Page 93: "Millstone or Milestone" by Peter J. Henniker-Heaton, reprinted by permission of the author and *The Christian Science Sentinel*. © 1966 by The Christian Science Publishing Society.

Page 94: "Gerard, the Giraffe" by Ethel Jacobson, reprinted by permission of the author and *The Christian Science Monitor*. © 1959 by The Christian Science Publishing Society.

Page 101: "The Park" by James S. Tippett from *Crickety Cricket! The Best-Loved Poems of James S. Tippett*. Pictures by Mary Chalmers. Text © 1973 by Martha K. Tippett. Used with the permission of Harper & Row, Publishers, Inc.

Page 110: "Geography" by Eleanor Farjeon. Copyright 1938 by Eleanor Farjeon. © renewed 1966 by Gervase Farjeon. From *Poems for Children* by Eleanor Farjeon. Copyright 1951 by Eleanor Farjeon. Reprinted by permission of J. B. Lippincott Company.

Page 115: "As a Little Child" by Mildred L. Hocker, reprinted by permission of the author and *The Christian Science Sentinel*. © 1962 by The Christian Science Publishing Society.

The author and publisher have exerted the greatest effort to locate copyright owners on all materials included in this volume. If there is anyone else who owns copyrights on any materials included herein, we will be most grateful to learn of it and will include proper acknowledgements in the next printing of this book.

ACKNOWLEDGEMENTS

I am most grateful for the fine work of my Italic students over the past 20 years, which has proven beyond dispute that Italic handwriting is indeed easy to learn, can be mastered by everyone, that it is fast, more readable, and tidier than the traditional commercial cursive, and that it is often beautiful.

Samples of the work of these students abound in the illustrations in this book.

I am also most grateful to Georgianna Dickinson of Salinas High School, Salinas, California, and to Karen Haslag of St. Charles School, San Francisco, California, for the imaginative work they are doing with their students. The samples of their students' work included in this book will give young people ideas of how they can spend many joy-filled hours doing artistic things with their pens. This is the beginning of creative calligraphy.

Grateful acknowledgement is due to all of my friends, teachers, and critics who have helped pave the way for such a volume as this.

To Will Norman for his lesson in simple pen decoration.

To Joseph Di Spigno, who engaged me to train his faculty at Fort Salonga School, Kings Park, L. I., where a very fine experiment in Italic handwriting is being conducted. The entire 600-pupil student body of Fort Salonga School is learning Italic, and the other Kings Park Schools are the control group, being trained in the customary commercial cursive. Samples of the Italic students' work are seen in this book, identified by "Kings Park, L.I., N.Y."

Last, but not least, my loving gratitude goes to my wife, Joanne, and to Lynn and Melissa, my daughters, each of whom has graciously given up some claims to my time, and has given wonderful assistance so that this book could be completed.

Macmillan Publishing Co., Inc.
866 Third Avenue, New York, N.Y. 10022
Collier Macmillan Canada, Ltd.

Library of Congress Cataloging in Publication Data
Eager, Fred.
   Italic handwriting for young people.
   SUMMARY: Introduces basic techniques of italic handwriting.
   1. Writing, Italic—Juvenile literature.
[1. Writing, Italic. 2. Penmanship] I. Title.
Z43.E117 1978b   745.6'197   78-1945
ISBN 0-02-079960-8 pbk.

Third Printing 1979

Printed in the United States of America

TABLE OF CONTENTS

COURSE OUTLINE FOR ITALIC HANDWRITING FOR YOUNG PEOPLE

This course outline recommends weekly goals for a student to set for himself as he is working through this book, or for a teacher to set for a class. When each item is completed, a check can be recorded on the line by the item number.

Each lesson should take about one week, except where otherwise indicated. This weekly session will prove particularly useful for an Italic Club which meets once or twice weekly.

LESSON I: Introduction; Italic Shapes; First Meeting
___ 1. Study beginning pages of book and do writing at top of page 8.
___ 2. Pages 10-12. Study these pages by tracing (writing on the model in the book), copying it next to the model, then on your own paper. (Use notebook paper with 3/8" spacing.)

LESSON II: Italic Shapes, contd. (Start this lesson after one week)
___ 3. Pages 13-16

LESSON III: Italic Shapes, contd. (After two weeks)
___ 4. Pages 17-20

LESSON IV: Italic Shapes, contd. (After three weeks)
___ 5. Pages 21-22. Study these pages very carefully.
___ 6. Page 23: Write the alphabet, 3 of each letter, underline your best of each letter (a<u>a</u>a, bb<u>b</u>, <u>c</u>cc, etc.)
___ 7. Pages 24, 25. Study the common faults and compare your alphabet of No. 6 with them, then practice the letters that need it most.

LESSON V: Review of Letter Shapes. (After 4 weeks)
___ 8. Pages 26, 27. Practice any of these pages that your analysis in No. 7 shows are necessary.
___ 9. Page 28. Copy this page as carefully as possible.
___ 10. Page 29. Analyze your work for good shapes, even slant and even spacing, and decide whether to review or to go on.

LESSON VI: Smaller Alphabets & Capitals (After 5 wks)
___ 11. Pages 30-34

LESSON VII: Capitals contd. (After 6 weeks)
___ 12. Pages 35-38

LESSON VIII: Fun with Italic Handwriting (After 7 wks)
___ 13. Pages 39-41. Practice these reversibles. Use them around one of the poems in Lesson VI or VII.
___ 14. Pages 42-44. Study these for ways to vary your practice.
___ 15. Page 45. Decide whether your shapes, slant and spacing need review, or whether you should continue.

LESSON IX: Diagonal Joins. Each of these units should take about one week.
___ 16. Pages 46-50 (After 8 weeks)
___ 17. Pages 51-55 (After 9 weeks)
___ 18. Pages 56-60 (After 10 weeks)
___ 19. Pages 61-65 (After 11 weeks)
___ 20. Pages 66-70 (After 12 weeks)
___ 21. Pages 71-75 (After 13 weeks)

LESSON X: Design a Greeting Card
___ 22. Using pages 74 or 75, or a poem of your own selection, design a greeting card, using a black nylon-tipped pen. Have about 50 printed by your local printer and send them to your friends.

LESSON XI: Learn to Use the Broad Edged Pen (After 15 weeks)
___ 23. Pages 76-86. (You should wait a while before trying to do arrangements like those on pages 77-80.)

LESSON XII: Review the Book, using Broad Edged Pen. Each unit should take about one week.
___ 24. Pages 30-33, 87. (After 16 weeks)
___ 25. Pages 35, 37, 38, 88. (After 17 weeks)
___ 26. Pages 39, 46-48, 89. (After 18 weeks)
___ 27. Pages 49, 50, 90, 52-54, 91. (After 19 wks)
___ 28. Pages 56, 59, 92, 62, 93. (After 20 weeks)
___ 29. Pages 63-66, 94. (After 21 weeks)
___ 30. Pages 68, 70, 73, 95 (Repeat page 95 until it is the best you can do.) (After 22 weeks)

LESSON XIII: Smaller Size with Pencil (After 23 wks)
___ 31. Pages 96-98
___ 32. Do many quotations and other writing in this size (5 to 10 pages).

LESSON XIV: The Medium Pen (After 24 weeks)
___ 33. Pages 99-102
___ 34. Many pages of other writing. (5-10 pages)

LESSON XV: More with the Medium Pen (After 25 wks)
___ 35. Pages 103-106
___ 36. Many more pages of writing.

LESSON XVI: Simple Flourished Capitals (After 26 wks)
___ 37. Pages 107-110 (Remember the Daily Warm-up)
___ 38. Many more pages of writing.

LESSON XVII: Building Speed (After 27 weeks)
___ 39. Pages 111-112 (Remember the Warm-up)
___ 40. Much additional daily practice on speed
___ 41. Copy some passages of your own choosing.

LESSON XVIII: Introducing the Two Modes of Italic Handwriting (After 28 weeks)
___ 42. Pages 113 & 114 (Calligraphic Mode only), 115.
___ 43. Find more passages to copy in this mode.

LESSON XIX: The Cursive Mode (After 29 weeks)
___ 44. Pages 113, 114, 116.
___ 45. Find more passages to copy.

LESSON XX: CONCLUSION (After 30 weeks)
___ 46. Prepare a piece to show the best you can do for display. Work on one quotation over and over until it is your best. Display of the students' work for all to enjoy.

INTRODUCTION AND INSTRUCTIONS

You can teach yourself Italic Handwriting from a book. I taught myself completely from books and from suggestions from experts whom I wrote for the first six years. Then I studied with one of the experts, Prof. Lloyd J. Reynolds. The suggestions and lessons helped me to _see_ things that I had missed in my study of the books themselves. Later Sheila Waters helped me with some of the fine details of Italic and I learned more from observation, practice, experimentation and teaching.

I have been writing books to include all the things I've learned so that students could teach themselves without the help of a teacher. Many have done this very well, but it is really _easier_ with the help of a teacher for these reasons:

A student will usually work harder when he has an appointment with a teacher for a lesson, and has been assigned a certain amount of work to have finished by that time. One who works by himself will be apt to "put it off until tomorrow."

A student may feel that he is following the directions very carefully and patiently, but there may be something he doesn't see; or he may be trying to go too fast...or too slow...or skipping something very important...or making something very important that really isn't, and so on. In any of these cases, the aid of a teacher can help a student save himself from wasting hours of wrong practice or, as I call it, "unpractice"!

The two greatest dangers facing any student of Italic, whether he is with a teacher or whether he is by himself are these:

HE'S TOO GOOD! What he does with a pencil or pen is so much more beautiful and perfect than anything he has ever done before, and he is so pleased with himself that he loses the ability to see his little mistakes and even the big ones.

HE'S TOO IMPOSSIBLY CLUMSY, AWKWARD, and just can't make any copies look like the model...so he's all ready to give up...out of patience...unhappy.

You can see that if a wise teacher were around, either of these students would soon be shown the truth of things; would be shown that he shouldn't waste time thinking about himself: too good OR too bad; that he should just get busy doing the best he can every moment of his practice, always be glad if he can make it look better each day than it looked the day before, and always be looking for ways to make it better right now.

REMEMBER:

A completely satisfied student can learn no more—he's dead.

A completely _dissatisfied_ student is drowning in self-pity and just wanting comfort...he might as well be dead!

Stay alive and be neither too satisfied nor too discouraged! Ever! Soon people will love the beauty you are creating...but still don't let it go to your head! There's much more to learn! When you've mastered everything in this book and are doing it really well, start looking for more books. Go to the library, book store, or art store. You might be ready to work with my book for adults: _The Italic Way to Beautiful Handwriting._ It has many more fancy things that are fun to do. After that look up other books on Italic Handwriting and on Calligraphy.

The method of trace-and-copy learned in this book can be applied to other alphabets, but please don't be in a hurry to get to them until you have mastered Italic well first.

Have fun! Work hard! And enjoy!

HOW TO USE THIS BOOK:

ALWAYS study the model by writing with your pencil _directly_ _on_ the model. Then, take the test! See if you have really learned the model, and copy it in the space next to it. The model is the teacher. Tracing it is your lesson. Copying next to it in the space provided is the test. Use a soft pencil (No. 1 or No. 2).

When you come to a page which does not have spaces for copying...such as a poem, or something else to copy, this is a 'BIG TEST'. Now try to copy this on your own paper, using a Guide Sheet in the back of the book under your paper without tracing the model. Sometimes students like to do this copying on very thin paper. After copying the model they put the paper on the model. They can see the model through the paper and discover the things they did that are different from the model.

THE EDGED PEN

The edged pen is not only fun to use because it brings beauty to handwriting practice, but because it is of great value in helping to keep a fast writing readable. It acts as a control on the hand without slowing it down.

After you learn to use the edged pen, continue to practice both slow and fast writing without it.

The first part of this book is to be studied with a pencil, then after the broad pen is introduced, the entire book, starting with page 30 is to be done again with the edged pen.

TEACHERS AND PARENTS

This book is designed for use by eight-year-olds and up. Adults will find useful practice in its pages...more practice than they can find in any other work-book for Italic Handwriting.

It is hoped that the words above to my young friends will also be of assistance to you as you guide them in their adventures with Italic Handwriting.

BENEFITS OF ITALIC HANDWRITING

As a handwriting, Italic is simple, easy to teach, easy to learn, a real pleasure to study because of its beauty. Because of its simplicity it can be more readable even when written at fast speeds.

Italic Handwriting is a great introduction to discipline in the entire art field. In fact, it can help students develop self-discipline in all phases of their lives. Italic Handwriting helps children build a good self-image. The trace-and-copy method helps train the eyes to see shapes more clearly. It helps to develop eye-hand coordination which is necessary in all of the arts.

Italic Handwriting is probably the easiest art form in which a child can do something so well that it looks like a 'grown-up' did it. (Many times I have heard adults viewing the Italic Handwriting of children say, "I wish I could do that!")

(What adults don't know is that Italic Handwriting is much easier to learn than it looks, and that it is such tremendous fun all the way, that it is really worth the effort and patience and time involved.)

IS ITALIC HARD TO LEARN?

I am quite convinced that anyone who is intelligent, who is patient, who can follow directions carefully, and who really wants to, can teach himself Italic Handwriting successfully with most pleasing results; and that he then has a tool which he can apply to learning other calligraphic alphabets, should he be interested. I have seen it happen over and over again. What at first seemed fantastic has now become commonplace. And it brings much satisfaction to have some part in helping thousands discover that they do, indeed, have a talent for what Graily Hewett called, "Handwriting, Everyman's Craft."

RIGHT HAND POSITIONS

To find the natural, comfortable position of the hand for holding a pen or pencil, swing your hand comfortably by your side, as when you are walking. Lift your forearm from the elbow and turn your hand in the same direction as you would when shaking hands with someone, but DO NOT change the curve of the fingers from that natural swinging position. Now, holding the pencil in your other hand, slip it into your writing hand so that the part near the point slips through the gap between the thumb and index finger and rests lightly on the side of the middle finger in the curve between the tip and the first joint. The back end of the pencil should rest somewhere near the knuckle at the base of the index finger and never down at the base of the thumb. The tip of the index finger should be slightly nearer the tip of the pencil than the thumb. At no time should there be any angularity or cramping of the hand.

Position at a Desk

Traditional Pen Hold

Middle Finger Up

Hand in a Knot

You may find that your middle finger can slip up onto the pencil...touching the pencil with the side of the finger very near the corner of the finger nail. Then the middle finger is nearer the tip of the pencil than the index finger, but the rest of the fingers are still in their relaxed curve and in the same relationship to each other as before. This middle-finger-up position might help encourage development of wrist movement and reduce finger movement, so long as the grip is not a tight one.

At no time should the thumb be out beyond the other fingers nor cramped way back behind them.

LEFT HAND POSITIONS

The best position, which permits a left-handed writer to use the square (right-handed) pens in their full range of sizes or widths is this one. Left-handed writers who are not too set in their ways find this a very comfortable position. The hand position is the same as for the right-handed writers.

The Best Position

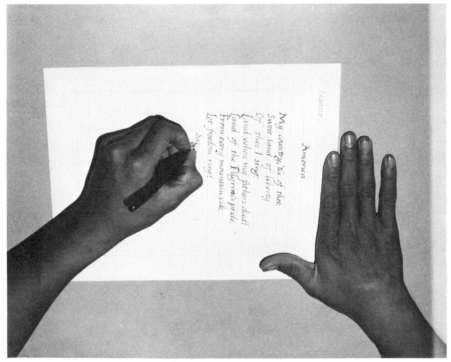

SPECIAL POSITIONS:
Here are other positions that have been used successfully by left-handed writers. Each illustration tells the type of pen the writer should use if he must adopt that position. In each of these special positions except the "wrap-around" position, the writer holds his elbow in towards his body and his wrist is flatter than in the right-handed position.

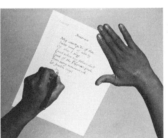

Position for Left/Hand Pen Usually the Easiest

Often the easiest position for left-handed writers who use Acute Oblique nibs (30° turn on nib), also called "Left-Handed nibs." These are available in only two sizes: Medium and fine.

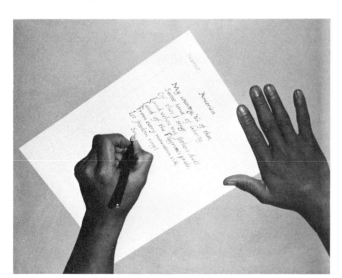

The best of the Special Positions: Writers use Left-Oblique nibs available for fountain pens in a wide range of sizes.

Try to avoid this one!

I generally try to switch writers accustomed to this position, because in this position all pen strokes are the reverse of what they should be: pushes are pulls, etc., and the writer must watch that he doesn't drag his hand over the wet ink. But I've known a few who have written successfully in this position. Square nib.

BEFORE AND AFTER & HOW DO YOU WRITE NOW?

These samples show the progress of children of all ages before and after studying Italic for varying lengths of time.

Please copy the following sentence three times in your present handwriting. Then you will have a sample with which you can compare your progress in this book.

Also, please clip into this book a page of schoolwork or other writing that shows your present handwriting for future comparison.

A quick brown fox jumps over the lazy dog.

_____   _____

_____   _____

_____

India is my country there are many people life living without parents There are on the road begging for money. There are many slum area in India India is the second largest city in There are

Beautiful
Beautiful faces are they that wear
The light of a pleasant spirit there;
Beautiful hands are they that do
Deeds that are noble, good and true;
Beautiful feet are they that go
Swiftly to lighten another's woe.
MC Guffey's Reader

Martin Norton, 15, after 4 months in America

A quick brown fox jumps over the lazy dog.
A quick brown fox jumps over the lazy dog.
A quick brown fox jumps over the lazy dog.

Youngster, let that show you what it is to be without a family, without a home, and without a country.... Stick by your family, boy, forget you have a self, while you do everything for them.... And for your country, boy, and for that flag, never dream a dream but of serving her as she bids you, though the service carry you through a thousand hells. No matter what happens to you, no matter who flatters you or who abuses you, never look at another flag, never let a night pass but you pray God to bless that flag. Remember, boy, that behind all these men you have to do with, behind officers and Government and people even, there is the Country Herself, your Country, and that you belong to Her as you belong to your own mother. Stand by her, boy, as you would stand by your mother!
From "The Man Without a Country" by Edward Everett Hale
Scott Maddock scripsit

Eighth Grader after 15 weeks, Greenwich, Conn.

A quick brown fox jumps over the lazy dog.
A quick brown fox jumps over the lazy dog.
A quick brown fox jumps over the lazy dog.

Frances Tielman   4-9-

A quick brown fox jumps over the lazy dog.
A quick brown fox jumps over the lazy dog.
A quick brown fox jumps over the lazy dog.
A quick brown fox jumps over the lazy dog.
A quick brown fox jumps over the lazy dog.

Increase in speed by 7th Grader from 75 to 85 letters per minute after 20 weeks of Italic study
Grand Island, N.Y.

A quick brown fox jumps over the lazy dog
A quick brown fox jumps over the lazy dog
A quick brown fox jumps over the lazy dog

But it was not its size that now impressed my companions; it was the knowledge that seven hundred thousand pounds in gold lay somewhere buried below its spreading shadows. The thought of the money as they drew nearer, swallowed up their previous terrors. Their eyes burned up in their heads; their feet grew speedier

David Whitaker, 12th Grade, after several weeks

A quick brown fox jumps
over the lazy dog.

A quick brown fox jumps over
the lazy dog.

A quick brown fox jumps
over the lazy dog.

A quick brown fox jumps
over the lazy dog.

Old Obadiah, he jumped in the fire.
The fire was so hot he jumped in the pot.
The pot was so black he jumped in a crack.
The crack was so shallow he jumped in the tallow.
The tallow was so soft he jumped in the loft
The loft was so high he jumped in the sky.
The sky was so blue he jumped in the glue,
And there he was stuck and we are stuck too.
                    How about you?

Martin Schooping, 6th Grade, before and after
30 weeks of Italic Club. Grand Island, N. Y.

The Eagle
He clasps the crag with crooked hands;
Close to sun in lonely lands,
Ringed with the azure world, he stands.

The wrinkled sea beneath him crawls;
He watches from his mountain walls.
And like a thunderbolt he falls.

Scot Goodrich, 6th Grade, after 3 months
Grand Island, N. Y.

Let every nation know
Wheather it shall pray any price
wishes us well or ill.
That
Bear
hardshi

Let every nation know

Whether it wishes us well or ill

That we shall pay any price,

Bear any burden, meet any hardship,

Support any friend, oppose any foe

To assure the survival and success

of liberty.

                    John F. Kennedy

Richard Hunt, 5th Grade, after 9 months
Kings Park, L. I., N. Y.

Let every nation know
Weather it wishes us well or ill
That we shall pay any price,
Bear and burden, meet any hardship

Let every nation know

Whether it wishes us well or ill

That we shall pay any price

Bear any burden, meet any hardship

Support any friend, oppose any foe

To assure the survival and success
of liberty

                    John F. Kennedy

Chris Ernandes, 5th Grade, after 9 months
Kings Park, L. I., N. Y.

A quick brown fox jumps over
dog a quick brown fox jump
lazy dog a quick brown fox j
the lazy dog a quick brown f

William Holbert, 9th Grade, mastered both
Calligraphic & Cursive Modes of Italic
Handwriting in one semester. Greenwich, Conn.

This I beheld, or dreame
There spread a cloud of a
And underneath the clou
A furious battle, and men
Shocked upon swords and
hen staggered b
ing along the
"Had I a s

To give up a project because it looks as though you will
never succeed in achieving the goal is folly, because it is
impossible for you to know how close to the goal you are until
you have actually completed the work. It might be the very
next instant when all the work you have put into the project
will suddenly come into focus and the goal will be won! Or,
with a new point gained in your understanding of the work,
you will suddenly find all remaining toil much easier.

Use a soft pencil (No. 1 or No. 2) with a light touch. Later you will do pages 46 - 75 a second time with an edged Italic pen.

TRACE & COPY

Copy the models to see if you can do the letters by yourself.

Study the models by writing on them (Tracing them)

Start out very slowly. Don't worry about speed. That will come later. First learn the details of these simple shapes.

Don't be in a hurry. Patient, careful work now will bring wonderful rewards later.

Notice how points and curves slightly overlap the Guide Lines. This is a must!

Write <u>on</u> the model, then make your copy look just like the model, if possible.

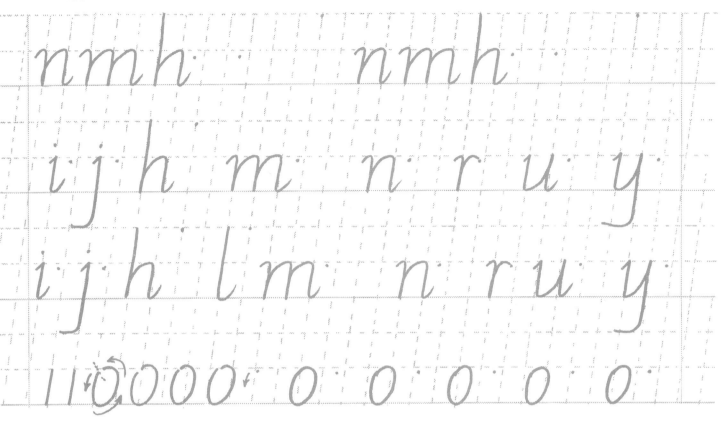

n m h   n m h

i j h   m   n   r u   y

i j h l m   n   r u   y

l l o o o o   o   o   o   o   o

The two-stroke <u>e</u> seems funny at first, but it is great for a good shape, and later
when it comes to making rhythmic joins. Start e with a curving down-stroke.

e e e e   e e   e   e   e   e   e   e

moon moon

hole   lonely

rule   money

Work carefully. Don't be in a hurry. Is your pencil hold relaxed or tight?

tttt   tt   tt   tin

Notice that t is not a TALL letter. t starts a little above the waist line.

ffff   ff   ff   fun

Ascender Line

Waist Line

ij l tf

Base Line

f starts midway between the waist line and the ascender line.
Both t and f cross just under, AND TOUCHING, the waist line.

Descender Line

For double ff's, draw the
two down strokes first, then
cross both with one stroke.
    Do the same for double tt's.

ff ff   ff

fit   lift   puff

little   mitt

muffle   lit

fine   fettle

m n r

Half-way

These are the "branching" letters, together with h, k, b and p. These letters all have a stroke that goes down to the base line, then <u>without lifting the pen,</u> retraces the stroke up half-way to the waist line. At that point it gradually branches out, and springs over to the waist line, then down. Keep the "ear" of <u>r</u> short so the next letter can be placed close enough without leaving a white hole in your writing line.

nnn nn nn n

mm mm m

men turn

mint trim

13

h k

hhh hh hh h

kkk kk kk kk k

hen   kneel

mouth   kit

hum   keen

For b follow carefully these points:

1. Straight down from the ascender line.
2. Retrace up WITHOUT LIFTING pen to a point half-way up to the waist line.
3. Branch out and up with a curving diagonal to
4. The point where the right side begins.
5. Straight down to the base line.
6. Push straight in to the stem.

DO NOT LIFT PENCIL WHILE WRITING b

Later you will replace the angles at points 4 and 6 with narrow curves, and the straight line (5) will become a flattish curve like the right side of o.

For p follow carefully these points:

1. Serif starts just below and moves to just above the waist line.
2. Sharply down to the descender line.
3. LIFT YOUR PENCIL!!
4. Put your pencil down again ON THE BASE LINE, NOT above it.
5. Retrace to a point half-way up to the waist line.
6, 7, 8, 9. Follow points 3, 4, 5, & 6 of the instructions for b (above)

b is written in one continous stroke WITHOUT lifting the pencil.

p is written in two strokes. The place where the pencil is placed for the second stroke is important: Right on the base line for an UP stroke that branches. This helps you get the same feel of branching as in the m, n, h, and b.

As you branch up with a curving diagonal try to remember the feel of n and h.

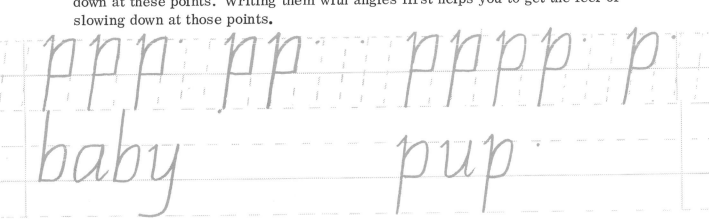

When you start to curve at the angles on the right side of b and p, you MUST slow down at these points. Writing them with angles first helps you to get the feel of slowing down at those points.

baby   pup

Does your hand feel cramped?
If so, shake it by your side with a rolling of your wrist until it is free again. Now go
ahead with your writing, but please don't hold the pencil so tight or press so hard on
the paper. Use a No. 1 pencil.

bubble put

blip help

bumper if

umpire it

purple pull

ʃʃʃʃʃ s fsfs fs

soft fist is

sleeps bust

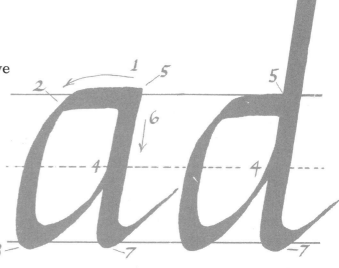

1. Push flat across the top from right to left.
2. Shoulder down rather squarely with a line that slants down to the base line.
3. Narrow turn and swing up with a diagonal curve
4. To a point half-way up to the waist line.
5. Then go straight up to the starting point. a, d, g, q all have this one-stroke pocket-like shape: ⟨⟩. For EACH letter the pencil should return to the starting point. Only the letter d has a lift which is AT this starting point. For letters a, g, and q, DO NOT LIFT THE PENCIL. Make them in one stroke.
6. Straight down to the base line. This makes your strokes look like the branching of b and p upside down.
7. End with a narrow curve matching the narrow curve at No. 3. Lift the pencil off the paper as you are doing this up stroke.

For d, points 1 - 4 are the same as for the other a-shapes, BUT

5. At 5, the starting point, LIFT your pencil. DO NOT lift it BEFORE you reach this point (No. 5).
6. Now place the pen on the ascender line at 6 and straight down to the base line, retracing the line from 5 to 4 on the way, and
7. End the same as point No. 7 in the a.

NOT ⟨⟩ ⟨⟩ ⟨⟩ ⟨⟩

DO NOT lift the pencil here, or the d looks shapeless: ⟨⟩

Start with angular corners. Practice them for some time, then, just slow down at these corners, making them narrow curves.

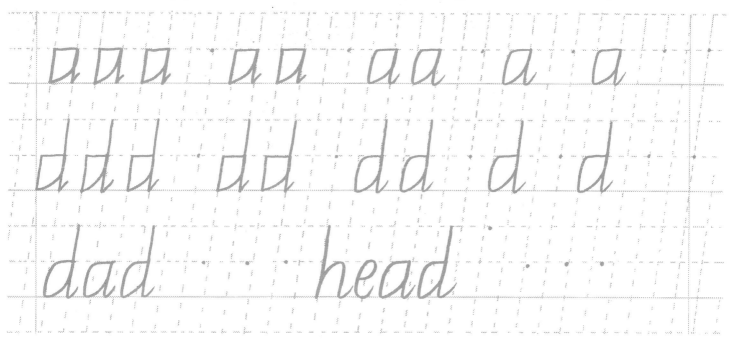

g g

g g g   g g   g g   g g

g g g   g g   g g   g

log   dog   go

egg   laugh

queen   cog

circus   cool

cloth   can't

cactus   cab

buffoon   of

fly   cry   eye

quiet   ice

request   by

crept   acid

Learn to make the last stroke of <u>v</u> and <u>w</u> turn in so they won't look like <u>r</u> which turns out.

vvv vv v v v

www w w w

van wave

wove view

xxx x v/x exit

zzz z z buzz

zero wax

six zip fuzz

i j u y

n m r

h k hb

p o o e

l t f s

a dd g

q c v

w x z

a   b   c

d d   e   f

g   h   i j

k   l m

n   o o   p

q   r s

t   u v

w   x   y z

abcdefghijklmnopq

rstuvwxyz

All of the letters are made in one stroke except those which have the figure two below them.

The pencil enters each of these letters with a sharp angle from the serif. On v, w, and x the sharp angle appears only after a join.

ijpuy (vwx)

The pencil enters each of these letters with a narrow curve.

mnrvwx

All letters which end in a serif do so with narrow lower curves except for these letters:

cote

aaabbbcccdddeeefff

Before proceeding, the student should "pass the alphabet" by writing each letter three times, underlining the one of the three he thinks is best. Use paper with 3/8" spacing like this.

ggghhhiiijjjkkklll

mmnopqrstuvwxyz

COMMON FAULTS I: Underlined letters are correct. Please draw arrows pointing to the faults in all of the other letters. Letters with faults are numbered to enable classes to discuss the faults. Check your alphabet with these to see if it is free from these faults.

1 2 3 4 5 6 7 8 9 10

11 12 13 14 15 16 17 18

19 20 21 22 23 24 25 26

27 28 29 30 31 32 33 34

35 36 37 38 39 40 41 42 43 44

COMMON FAULTS II

Now compare your alphabet with these to see if it is free from these faults.

r r n n n n n n

m m m m m m

h h h h h h h

k k k k k k k k

b b b b n p p p p

b b b b opp p p

nap   pup

bump   up

a a a a a a a

d d d d d d d

g g g g g g g

q q q q q q q

a a a a a a a

d d d d d d d

g g g g g g g

dad   gang

A quick brown fox

jumps over the lazy

dog. 11 22 2 2

33 3 44 4

55 5 66 6 77 7

88 8 99 9 00 0

Students should not go farther until:
1. Their letter shapes are like the models.
2. Their letters overlap the guide lines.
3. Their slant is consistent.
4. Their spacing is even.

When you learn to use the Broad Pen, you will do the following pages a second time with the pen, but you will copy poems starting on page 87 instead of <u>these</u> poems. The Course Outline on page 4 will help you know which pages to do next, and the notes at the bottom of these pages will also help you the second time around.

Now we work with the same alphabet in a smaller size. Remember that since the letters are smaller in height, they are also smaller in width so the proportion is the same.

aa a a bb b b cc c dd d d eee e e ff f

gg g g hh h ii i jj j kk k lll l mm m

m nn n oo o pp p p p qq q q q rr r

ss s tt t uu u vv v ww w xx x y z z

aaa bbb ccc ddd eeee fff

ggg hhh iii jjj kkk lll mmm

m nnn ooo ppp qqq rrr

sss ttt uuu vvv www w

xxx yyy zzz aa bb dd p

A A A A B B B C C C D D D

E E E F F F G G G G H H H I I

J J K K L L L M M M M N N

N O O O P P P Q Q Q R R R

S S T T T U U U V V V W W W

X X Y Y Y Z Z Z 1 1 1 2 2 2

2 3 3 3 4 4 4 5 5 5

6 6 6 7 7 7 8 8 8 8

9 9 9 12 34 56 78

From now on, all schoolwork should be written on special paper with spaces 5/32 to 3/16 inch between lines like on the other pages in this book or on regular notebook paper like this, with lines 3/8" apart. On this paper, write ½ space high. Ascenders on tall letters touch the line above while descenders like g, j, p go half-way down into the space below: abcdefghijklmn.

The letter f and capitals are 3/4 of a space high: A B C D E F G H I J. You write in every other space. Skip a line!

Now we are working for good letter shapes with even slant and spacing. NOT speed!

add · bank · dad · gate · race ·

place · dart · bark · farm ·

jar · jet · net · sell · yet · sled ·

keeping · meet · seeds · bean

clean · leave · eat · where ·

there · their · my · bit · chin ·

dip · pin · rib · white · write ·

nine · ice · fog · lock · pop ·

rock · box · broke · dope · hole

note · school · poor · moon ·

food · look · book · foot · hook ·

wood · should · could ·

would · corn · morning ·

store · out · mouse · house ·

found · duck · run · plus ·

must · always · snowing ·

work · sister · brother · dish ·

anything · different · dirty ·

closet · armies · navies · toast ·

Choose other spelling words to write (One page)

Watch the size of your capitals. They are 1-1/2 times the size of a in height.

A A A A A A A A A A A A A

Ann   Alice   Andrew

B B B B B B B B B B B B B

Bunny   Bart   Beverly

C C C C C C C C C C C C C

Charles   Carrie   Cam

D D D D D D D D D D D

Daniel   Debra   Dan

E E E E E E E E E E E

Evelyn   Eugene   Eric

F F F F F F F F F F F F

Floyd   Florence   Fran

G G G G G G G G G G G

Grace   Guy   Gloria

A   B   C   D   E   F   G   H

H H H H H H H H H H

Herman   Hilda

After doing this page for the second time (with the broad pen) do page 87

Trace the <u>odd</u>-numbered lines: trace a word, then <u>copy</u> it below, then the next word, etc. <u>Just copy</u> the <u>even</u> numbered lines on the line below <u>without</u> tracing. See if you can make them look like the model as much as those lines which you trace and copy.

1. A good reader may travel far, – in books.

2. A good story-teller makes many happy.

3. An honest man has a happy heart.

4. One who works hard accomplishes much.

5. In sleep we dream, but we have to be awake,

6.   to make dreams come true.

7. Sing a happy tune, and lighten your burdens,

8. A smile is one of the finest gifts we can give,

9.   yet it costs nothing.

II I I I I I I Izzie J J J J J

Jean Joan John

KK K K K K KK K K K K K K

Kathy Keith Karen

LL L L L L L L Lillian Lee

Lewis M M M M M

M M M M M M

Martin Meg Mary

N N N N N N N

Nan Nelly Neil

OO O O O O O O O O O O O

Ogg Oscar Oliver

P P P P P P P P P P P P P

Pamela Peter Paul

Q Q Q Q Q Q Q Q Q Q Q Q Q

Quincy R R R R R R R R

Ronald Rose Renee

After the second time, do pages 37 and 38 next.

HUMPTY DUMPTY

Humpty Dumpty sat on a wall:
Humpty Dumpty had a great fall.
All the king's horses and all the king's men
Couldn't put Humpty together again.

Lewis Carroll

BE LIKE THE BIRD

Be like the bird, who
Halting in his flight
On limb too slight
Feels it give way beneath him,
Yet sings,
Knowing he hath wings.

Victor Hugo

S S S S S S S S S S S S S S S S

Stanley   Sue   Stuart

T T T T T T Terry   Tom

U U U U U   Unice

V V V V V V V V

Vickie   Vernon   Vincent

W W W W W W W

W W W W W W

Wesley   Wanda

X X X X X X X X X X X

Xavier   Xantippe

Y Y Y Y Y Y Y Y Y Y Y Y

Yutang   Yul   Yvonne

Z Z Z Z Z Z Z Z Z

Zambezi   Zealand

Betsy   Patrick   Randy

Bill   Pat   Ricky   Bob

Evening Hymn

Now the day is over,
    Night is drawing nigh,
Shadows of the evening
    Steal across the sky.

Now the darkness gathers,
    Stars begin to peep;
Birds and beasts and flowers
    Soon will be asleep.

Through the lonely darkness,
    May the angels spread
Their white wings above me,
    Watching round my bed.

Mc Guffey's Second Reader

When students can write pages 34, 36, and 38 so well that they look very much like the models, they may learn to use the broad-edged pen beginning on page 72 for extra practice in addition to their regular work on the following pages, using a soft pencil.

After the second time do page 88

FUN WITH ITALIC HANDWRITING

Trace these reversible shapes and then copy them in the space below. Use them as borders around your poems and quotations (See page 41).

ititititititititititititititititititititititititititititi

Copy →

rv AVAVAVAVAV
→

Copy →

a or

av ecoecoecoecoecoecoecoec

dPdPdPdPdPdPdP or dPdPdPdPdPdPdP

d° qbqbqbqbqbqbqbqbqbqbq

q hhhhhhhhhhhhhhhh

sf hyhyhyhyhyhyhyhyhy
→

Yhyhyhyhyhyhyhyhyhy

gbgbgbgbgbgbgbgb jljljljljljljljljljlj
→

39

DESCRIPTION AND EXPLANATION OF PAGES 41-44 and 77-82

There are some fun things you can do with your Italic Handwriting. The only limits are your imagination, your artistic sense, and your good taste. Extravagant curlicues and gaudy colors are, of course, in bad taste.

The rule for decorating writing is that the message, the writing itself, is the most important thing. If your decoration overpowers or overshadows or detracts from this, then your result may be a virtuosic display of artistic talents very offensively wasted in frivolous and tasteless excess. Too much salt spoils the taste of otherwise excellent food. Too much sugar spoils some beverages and foods.

The answer is try everything, practice over and over and over until you find what is just right. Throw away all the bad tries and let people see your best.

FROM THE National Competition Survey Exhibit

All of the colorful pieces illustrated on pages 42-44 and 77-80 were entered in the National Competition Survey Exhibit which was jointly sponsored by Italimuse Inc. and Pentalic Corp. in the spring of 1977.

Pages 42-44 show the work of students in 3rd and 4th grades at St. Charles School in San Francisco, under the tutelage of Karen Haslag.

Pages 77-80 show the work of students in Salinas High School, taught by Georgianna Dickinson. Her students' work is characterized by its freshness, originality, and vitality. It will give our readers some glimpses at a few of the hundreds of possibilities which inventive students can develop in arranging a text.

Sources of other materials on this page and pages 81-82 are individually credited with the examples.

SIMPLE THINGS TO DO

Page 41 shows the author's application of a little color and a decorative border to a quotation. Here are some of the decorative things the 3rd and 4th graders at St. Charles School do:

Have drawings around their quotations, illustrating the quotation or poem.

Fill in some of the inside of the letter shapes. This, by the way, is an excellent way to become conscious of the interior shapes of your letters. Remember, the inside shapes of a, d, g, q, and of b and p should be similar (b and p inverted and reversed: turn the page upside down to see if they match your a, d, g, q shapes).

Write the quotation lightly with pencil first, then go over the writing with bright-colored nylon-tipped markers. Use different colors for different words.

The most extravagant use of color over pencil was done in this manner: alternate two colors through one letter, changing four or five times between the two colors, then changing to two other colors on the next letter, etc. The effect is a very colorful mosaic and the task fascinates children while they study the letters in detail. Miss Haslag used this method in addressing a brown envelope using only two colors. Melissa Eager, 8, 4th Grade, illustrates this way in an alphabet. I don't believe this would work on writing smaller than 1/4 inch for the x-height, but you may like to try it.

Color changes on these pages can be detected by the changes from black to grey and by the varying grey tones in the reproductions.

How is Int.
organized, (
one subject ar
The poetry a
separate secti

How many
parts in the
table of conter
at the back of

What helps
contents, prly
literary termi
list by types
your reading
literature secti

3454 Sandy Beach
Grand Island, New
April 29, 1970

Dear Mr. Eager,
I like Italic Writing because it
improved my writing. My writing u:
to be very messy. Now it is very beautif.

It has also improved my personalit
I have learned to be patient and keep
on trying.

It is also fun seeing the changes i
my writing. I am very proud of m
writing now.

Sincerely yours,
Susan Lorimer

Dear Mr. Eager,
Merry Christmas! I hope that this bicentennial year was a happy one for you and your family. I have been very busy with my school-work; the curriculum for chemical engineering is very demanding. So far things have been going well. Last summer I had a good job with Du Pont - and I believe I will be back there again this coming summer. Paul is graduating from the Univ. of Texas this spring, I really can't believe it.

In spite of my busy schedule, I have managed to stay in the symphonic band at A&M. None of us are music majors, A&M has no music program. All of us enjoy music. We have received the great honor of being invited

Progress of one student who started in 7th Grade,
after 7 months, and then as a sophomore in college,
using Italic for practical purposes.

WHATSOEVER ye do,
do all to the glory of God.
ST. PAUL

HEREIN is my Father
GLORIFIED,
that ye bear much fruit.
So shall ye be my disciples.
CHRIST JESUS

Little Nanny Etcout
In a white petticoat
The longer she stands,
The shorter she grows.

Sarah Cawaring
9, 4th Grade

Gifts

Give me goods.
Give me sweets.
Give me something good to eat!

Norma

Norma Oropera
8, 3rd Grade

Fuller information and credit for these pages is given on page 40

Where's little pinky?
Here I am.
Where's little thumby?
Here I am.
Where are all the little fingers?
Here we are.
Making a little bubble stars

By Llezelle

Llezelle Augustin
8, 3rd Grade

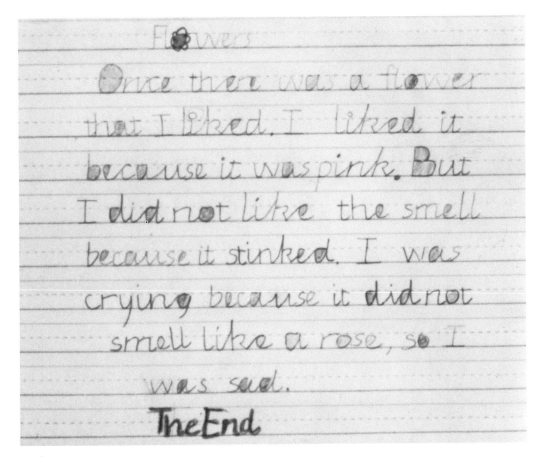

Flowers
Once there was a flower that I liked. I liked it because it was pink. But I did not like the smell because it stinked. I was crying because it did not smell like a rose, so I was sad.
The End

Veronica Sol
8, 3rd Grade

I wonder if thunder
Frightens a bee,
A mouse in her house,
A bird in a tree,
A hare or a bear,
A fish in the sea?
Not me !

Marisela Parra
8, 3rd Grade

Martha Carrillo
9, 4th Grade

Crawl caterpillar
Crawl as you will
someday you'll awake
and Soar !

Melissa Eager, 8, Wilton, Conn.

abcdefghijklmnopq
rstuvwxyz

No joins should be learned until:
  1. Letter shapes are good, with lower serifs
     having narrow curves: ıʅ ıʅ NOT ı or ᴗ
  2. Slant is consistent.
  3. Spacing is even.

THE WONDERFUL 2-STROKE e

To start our study of joins, we study all the possibilities the 2-stroke e gives us.
    1. It is easy to swing any letter up to the beginning point of the 2-stroke e without breaking the rhythm. 2. With the 2-stroke e it is much easier to keep the eye of the e open. (The looped one-stroke e always wrecks the spacing and rhythm, the eye closes up too easily, and its influence on the hand is to make it feel like looping everything.)

e e e e e e e e e e

keen   been

e e e e ee   ee ee ee

feet   seed wheel

ie ie ie ie pie pie pie

chief chief field

ee ee eee eee tree tree

fee ie ie ie ie chief chief

me me heel heel

sleep sleep deer deer

need need need

46

The aim here is to learn to join and to write with rhythm, NOT YET SPEED.
Work for a good, flowing, swinging rhythm. Swing it along!

uuu uuu · uuu · uuu · uuu · uuu

nn nn · nn · nn · nn · nn ·

mmm mmm · mmm · mmm

nnn nnn · nnn · nnn · nnn

mumu mumu · mumu ·

mumu · mumu · mumu

nono no · nono · no · nono · no ·

quote quote · quote · quote ·

built built · built · built

ue ue ue ue · ue · ue · ue · ue ·

blue blue · blue · blue · blue

fuel fuel · fuel · fuel · fuel

mule mule · mule · mule ·

hut hut · hut · hut · hut

hello hello · hello · hello

us us us · us us · us · us · us · us ·

must must · must · must

cup cup · cup · cup · cup · cup

mitt mitt · mitt · mitt · mitt

built built · built · built

umum umum · umum ·

unit unit · unit · unit

mile mile · mile · mile ·

mitten mitten · mitten ·

mummy · mummy ·

dump dump · dump · dump

neither neither · neither ·

lump lump · lump · lump

nest nest · nest · nest · nest ·

meet meet · meet · meet ·

kept kept · kept · kept · kept

number · number · number

home home · home · home ·

amen amen · amen · amen

avenue avenue · avenue · avenue

tune tune · tune · tune ·

this this · this · this · this · this

then then · then · then · then

new new · new · new · new ·

distill distill · distill ·

After the second time do page 89

nm nm · nm · nm · nm · nm ·
mm · mm · mm · mm ·
mumu · mumu · mumu
mi mi · mi · mi mi · mi · mi
mj · mj mj · mj · mj · mj ·
mo mo · mo · mo · mo · mo ·
mo me · me · me · me · me ·
ms ms · ms · ms · ms · ms ·
mt mt · mt · mt · mt · mt ·
mv mv · mv · mv · mv · mv ·
mw · mw · mw · mw · mw ·
ai · aim · aim · aim · ·
ao · chaos · chaos · chaos ·
ap · ape · ape · ape · ape ·
as · ash · ash · ash · ash ·
ask · ask · ask · ask · ask ·
at · ate · ate · ate · ate · ate ·
au · auto · auto · auto · auto
av · have · have · have ·
aw · away · away ·

ci city city city city

ct act act act act act

do door door door door

ds fads fads fads fads

du du dump dump

ce ce cell cell cell cell

ccccc ccccc ccccc ccccc

de de deed deed deed

he he he he he he he

li lie lie lie lie lie lie

ke keep keep keep keep

le let let let let let let

need need need need

ei ei eight eight eight

ej eject eject eject eject

eo eon eon eon eon eon eon

es nest nest nest nest

ev ever ever ever ever ever

ew blew blew blew blew

ex exit exit exit exit exit

After the second time do page 90

Trace a line and copy it below, then just copy the next line, trace & copy the next one and so on. See if the lines you just copy are as good as the ones you trace & copy.

1.   Keep on trying! Don't give up! You might

2. almost have it. Keeping at it may be the

3. only difference between success and failure.

4.   Love one another by being thoughtful,

5. kind, polite, and considerate instead of hurt-

6. ing others or causing trouble. Trouble comes

7. from selfishness,— nothing more than exag-

8. gerated thoughts of one's self.

9.   Be ye kind one to another.
                              Paul

ey eye eye eye eye ey eye

ue blue blue blue blue

hut hut hut hut hut

nip nip nip nip nip nip

else else else else else else

belt belt belt belt belt belt

miss miss miss miss

help help help help help

always always always

no no no no no no no no

yes yes yes yes yes yes yes

the the the the the the

bus bus bus bus bus bus

cup cup cup cup cup cup

Joins to: r m n x

mr mr mr mr mr mr

mn mn mn mn mn

mm mm mm mm

mx mx mx mx mx mix

are   are   are   are   are   are
an   an   an   an   an   an
am   am   am   am
axle   axle   axle   axle
imp   imp   imp   imp
her   her   her   her   her   her
hen   hen   hen   hen   hen
empty   empty   empty
exit exit   exit   exit   exit   exit
flux   flux   flux   flux   flux
air   air   air   air   air   air
dinner   dinner
ban   ban   ban   ban
number   number
nine   nine   nine   nine
shine   shine shine   shine
summer   summer
chump   chump   chump
men   men   men   men
limb   limb   limb   limb

Joins To: a c d g q

ma ma ma ma ma

mc mc mc mc mc

md md md md

mg mg mg mg mg

mq mq mq mq mq

mud mud mud mud

nag nag nag nag

can can can can

daisy daisy daisy

each each each each

hand hand hand

mail mail mail mail

nap nap nap nap nap

accept accept accept

neck neck neck neck

uncle uncle uncle

add add add add

badge badge badge

laughs laughs

After the second time do page 91

A Kite

I often sit and wish that I
Could be a kite up in the sky,
And ride upon the breeze and go
Whichever way I chanced to blow.

Anonymous

Say Well and Do Well

Say well and do well
   End with one letter;
Say well is good,
   Do well is better.

Anonymous

Find more short poems and copy them.
Write slowly, form your letters carefully.
Always give the author's name. In the
corner write: Written by
with your name.

55

leg leg leg leg leg leg

bud bud bud bud bud

ugly ugly ugly ugly

acquaint acquaint

equal equal equal

age age age age age

aid aid aid aid aid

aquarium aquarium

cat cat cat cat cat

cider cider cider

dad dad dad dad

dear dear dear dear

midget midget

egg egg egg egg egg

equal equal equal

insect insect insect

ladder ladder ladder

baggy baggy baggy

paddle paddle paddle

sudden sudden

After the second time, do page 59 next

Tweedledum and Tweedledee
  Agreed to have a battle;
For Tweedledum said Tweedledee
  Had spoiled his nice new rattle.

  Just then flew down a monstrous crow,
    As black as a tar barrel,
  Which frightened both the heroes so,
    They quite forgot their quarrel.

                    Lewis Carroll

Again, trace and copy word by word, then just copy the next line, alternating lines through the page.

Home on the Range

Oh, give me a home where the buffalo roam,

Where the deer and the antelope play,

Where seldom is heard a discouraging word,

And the skies are not cloudy all day.

Home, home on the range,

Where the deer and the antelope play,

Where seldom is heard a discouraging word,

And the skies are not cloudy all day.

Joins From: o f t

noi   noi   noi   noi   noi
noe   noe   noe   noe   noe
noon   noon   noon
nose   nose   nose   nose
now   now   now   now   now
annoy   annoy   annoy
mouth   mouth   mouth
money   money   money
song   song   song   song
nfi   unfit   unfit   unfit
ff ff ff fluffy   fluffy   Fluffy
tin   tin   tin   tin   tin tin
ft ft   after   after   after
none   none   none   none
fox fox fox fox fox fox
boat   boat   boat   boat
foggy   foggy   foggy   foggy
tail   tail   tail   tail   tail
facts   facts   facts   facts

After the second time do page 92

Riddle: What Am I?

They chose me from my brothers:
"That's the nicest one," they said,
And they carved me out a face and put a
Candle in my head;
And they set me on the doorstep.
Oh, the night was dark and wild,
But when they lit the candle, then I
Smiled!

Dorothy Aldis

Weekly Assignment:

1 aaabbbcccdddeeefffggghhhiiijjjkkklllmmm
nnnooopppqqqrrrsssttttuuuvvvwwwxxxyyy
zzz AAABBBCCCDDDEEEFFFGGGHHHIII
JJJKKKLLLMMMNNNOOOPPPQQQRRR
SSSTTTUUUVVVWWWXXXYYYZZZ
1112222333344455566677788899900

2 Write one sentence slowly, without joins:
A quick brown fox jumps over the lazy dog.

3 Spelling words written rhythmically with joins,
one line of each word (1 page per week):
summer summer summer summer

4 One quotation carefully written.

5 Sample of regular schoolwork.

6 Progress in your handwriting book.

Joins From: r   v   w

nri nri   nri   nri   nre   nre   nre

rich·   rich·   rich·   rich·   rich·

read·   read·   read·   read·   read

art·   art·   art art·   art·   art·

crumb·   crumb·   crumb·

narrow·   narrow·   narrow·

terrible·   terrible·   terrible·

visit·   visit·   visit·   visit·

vent·   vent·   vent·   vent·

bravo·   bravo·   bravo·   bravo·

very·   very·   very·   very·   very·

envy·   envy·   envy·   envy·   envy

wind·   wind·   wind·

wood·   wood·   wood·   wood·

swung·   swung·   swung·

dwarves dwarves·   dwarves·

river·   river·   river·   river·

wrap·   wrap·   wrap·   wrap·

wave·   wave·   wave·   wave·

After the second time do page 93

Special practice on d

o o d o d d d d d d d d d d d d d d

dad dad   dad   dad   dad

dandy   dandy   dandy

add   add   add   add   add

muddy   muddy

eddy   eddy   eddy   eddy

COPY:

My name is Donald (Girls write Donna).

On hot days I go down for a dip in the pool and dive into the deep end. Eddy swims and dives with me.

After swimming one day we had a big duck dinner and drank a delicious date-flavored drink.

I have a dark brown dog. He plays with Daddy and me. We named him Digger for he digs up old bones other dogs have buried.

FILL THE ENTIRE PAGE by copying the line you trace all the way across the page. This practice is the most important one for studying and improving your slant and spacing. After this page is completed, keep practicing with letters and words in this same way until you KNOW that you have excellent slant and spacing.

iiiuiiiuaiiiu　iiiu　uiiiu　iiiu

iiiniiiniiiniiiniiim　iiin

iiinuiiinuiiinu　iiinuiiinu

iiiaiiiaiiia　iiibiiib

iiiciiiciiic　iiidiiid

iiieiiieiiie　iiifiiifiiif

iiigiiigiiig　iiihiiih

iiiiiiii　iiijiiij

iiikiiik　iiiliiil

iiimiiim　iiiniiin

iiioiiio　iiipiiip

iiiqiiiq　iiiriiir

iiisiiis　iiitiiit

iiiuiiiu　iiiviiiv

iiiwiiiw　iiixiiix

iiiyiiiy　iiiziiiz

iiibrightiiibright

iiiplantiiiplant

iiiletteriiiletter

iiibillowiiibillow

Special practice on p

p p p . p . pp . p . p . p . p . p . p . p . p . p . p . p .

people   people   people

pump   pump   pump

puppy   puppy   puppy

hippopotamus

apples   apples   apples

COPY:

My name is Paul (girls write: Paula)

I raise guppies in my fish pond. The

only trouble I have is that my puppy, named

Pups, likes guppies. I try to keep him away

by playing ping-pong with people. (Pups

likes ping-pong even better than barking at

guppies.) If I put pepper on the pond Pups looks

for paper popcorn. He loves to play with pink

paper popcorn. I don't know why pepper on the

pond reminds Pups of pink paper popcorn.

Summary of Rhythmic Diagonal Joins

FROM: a c d e h i k l m n u

TO: a c d e g i j m n o p q r s
t u v w x y NOT TO: b f h k l z

mn mn · mn · mn · mn · mn ·

mm mm · mm · mm ·

mu mu · mu mu ·

mi mi · mine · mine ·

me me me · me · me · me · me ·

ms ms aims · aims · aims

mn mn · autumn ·

mix mix · mix 1 mix · mix ·

mend mend · mend ·

ma ma · man · man ·

nc nc · anchor · anchor ·

nd nd · and · and · and ·

ng ng · sing · sing · sing ·

md md · mud · mud · ·

ag ag · nag · nag · nag ·

family · family

After the second time do page 94

The Swallow

Fly away, fly away, over the sea,
Sun-loving swallow, for summer
is done.
Come again, come again, come
back to me,
Bringing the summer and bringing
the sun.

Christina Georgina Rossetti

Summary of Rhythmic Horizontal Joins
FROM: f o t v r w
TO: a c d e g i j m n o p q
r s t u v w x y

moo moo moon · moon · ·

mop · mop · mop · mop ·

nose nose · nose · nose · nose ·

not not · not · not · not · not

noun noun · noun · noun ·

now now · now · now · now

fine fine · fine · fine · fine

after after · after · after · after

enter enter · enter · enter ·

none none · none · none ·

afraid afraid · afraid · afraid

nod nod · nod · nod · nod ·

unfair unfair · unfair ·

instant · instant · instant

row row · row · row · row ·

van van · van · van · van ·

After the second time, do pages 70 and 73 next

Thanksgiving

For flow'rs that bloom about our feet,
For tender grass, so fresh, so sweet,
For song of bird and hum of bee,
For all things fair we hear or see,
For blue of stream and blue of sky,
For pleasant shade of branches high,
For fragrant air and cooling breeze,
For beauty of the blooming trees,
Father in heav'n, we thank Thee.

Ralph Waldo Emerson

Rhythmic Join Practice

aim   age   and
day   dad   did
done   can   come
cat   cap   class
care   age   ask
ace   address   eel
corny   every   end
elbow   been   man
many   more   in
men   mud   me
make   moon
much   name
drum   mind   hand
him   here   map   home
heart   no   under   his
never   has   ham   her
hair   run   sang   boom
from   afraid   must
fun   dwarf   violin   visit

The lion and the unicorn
Were fighting for the crown,
The lion beat the unicorn
All about the town.

Some gave them white bread,
And some gave them brown;
Some gave them plum cake
And drummed them out of town.

Old nonsense rhyme

Bundles

A bundle is a funny thing,
It always sets me wondering;
For whether it is thin or wide
You never know just what's inside.

Especially on Christmas week,
Temptation is so great to peek!
Now wouldn't it be much more fun
If shoppers carried things undone?

John Farrar

More Rhythmic Join Practice

mix-up   poor   poor

boy   boy   light   light

lamp   lamp   lamp

let   let   leaf   leaf

lie   lie   letter   letter

kind   kind   fat   fat

address   address

keep   keep   kick   kick

key   key   kilometer

kilometer   keg   keg

kid   kid   cake   cake

ooze   ooze   oats   oats

otter   otter   tell   tell

took   took   table   table

far   far   fresh   fresh

free   free   fun   fun

five   five   train   train

still   still   fed   fed

swimmer   swimmer

After the second time do page 95

Dreidel Song
Twirl about, dance about,
Spin, spin, spin!
Turn, Dreidel, turn —
Time to begin!

Soon it is Hanukkah —
Fast, Dreidel, fast!
For you will lie still
When Hanukkah's past.

Ephraim Rosensweig

Cradle Hymn

Away in a manger,
No crib for a bed,
The little Lord Jesus
Lay down his sweet head;
The stars in the heavens
Looked down where he lay,
The little Lord Jesus
Asleep in the hay.

Martin Luther

PLAY WITH AN EDGED PEN

The first thing to get used to with an edged pen, is holding it in such a manner that the entire edge of the pen nib touches the paper all of the time. The ink flows down the crack and then out on the edge of the nib across the paper, giving a thick stroke. Without the full contact with the paper the ink does not flow properly.

The next problem is to learn to hold the edge of the pen always at a consistent angle of about 45° to the line of writing. Have fun with this page. Fill it with pen marks. If you can get the diagonal strokes at the angle shown you will soon write beautifully with the edged pen.

Touch the paper in many places with the edge of the pen and make dots:

Notice that the dots slant in different directions:
Can you now make all the dots slant this way: ?

Now make lower curves, skinny and fat:

Can you now make the lower curves end with a thin line going in this direction: ?

Now make upper curves:

Can you now start them always with a thin, slanting, diagonal up-stroke: ?

Now combine these strokes. Can you always start and end with thin diagonal up-strokes:

Now, free play, but try to always start and end with thin diagonal upstrokes:

Beautiful faces are they that wear The light of a pleasant spirit there; Beautiful hands are they that do deeds that are noble, good and true Beautiful feet are they that go swiftly to lighten another's woe McGuffey's Second Reader

Pam Stover
16, 11th Grade

Judy Hays
15, 10th Grade

Beautiful

Beautiful faces are they that wear The light of a pleasant spirit there; Beautiful hands are they that do Deeds that are noble, good and true; Beautiful feet are they that go Swiftly to lighten another's woe. —McGuffey's Second Reader

Fuller information and credit for these pages is given on page 40

Beautiful faces
are they that
wear

Beautiful hands
are they that
do

Beautiful feet
are they that
go

McGuffey's Second Reader

Beautiful

The light of a
pleasant spirit
there;

Deeds that are
noble, good &
true;

Swiftly to lighten
another's
woe.

Kathy Fleeman
17, 12th Grade

Jill McWhirter
14, 9th Grade

B eautiful
faces are they
that wear The light
of a pleasant spirit there;
Beautiful hands are they that do
BEAUTIFUL
McGuffey's Second Reader
Deeds that are noble, good and
true; Beautiful feet are
they that go Swiftly
to lighten
another's
woe

78

Beautiful

faces are they that wear
The light of a pleasant spirit there;
Beautiful hands are they that do
Deeds that are noble, good and true;
Beautiful feet are they that go
Swiftly to lighten another's woe.

McGuffey's Second Reader

Teresa Carey
17, 12th Grade

Stephanie Young
15, 10th Grade

79

Beautiful faces are they that wear
The light of a pleasant spirit there;
Beautiful hands are they that do
Deeds that are noble, good and true;
Beautiful feet are they that go
Swiftly to lighten another's woe.
McGuffey's Second Reader

Lisa Fukui
17, 12th Grade

Miroslava Magallan
15, 9th Grade

Beautiful faces are they that wear
The light of a pleasant spirit there;
Beautiful hands are they that do
Deeds that are noble, good, and true;
Beautiful feet are they that go
Swiftly to lighten another's woe.

McGuffey's Second Reader

Peggy Patrick
English

1. The donkey's ears are long.
2. The men's shoes are in the bas
3. My father's office is on the se
4. The girls' gym meets at 10 o'
5. The calves' mothers are in the
6. That is James's book on the tab
7. Have you read Lincoln's Getty
8. The winners' names are posted
9. The horses' tails were braided.
10. The elephants' trainer was

~~I like reading books. I like~~
I also ~~like~~ especially I
books such as Patton
I like soccer and bask

secretion- process by wich
chemical substances are proa

sensitivity- all living thin
the ability to detect and res
factors in their enviement calle

reproduction- life process by wi
produce more of their own ki

metabolism -all the life acti
performed by an organis

Grade 8+1
Sept. 16, 1960

A

Jim Herkimer
Lit.

Recollections

The doorbell rang. "It's for you, Jimmy," said
my mother. Four thirty after school and I was at my
desk doing homework! A neighbor boy, five years
younger than myself was at the door. He asked, as was
his daily custom, if I could come out and play with
him. My mother said to me, "He's too little for you."
Yet I stopped and remembered that when I was
little, I liked to go down the street and see an older
boy too! He was always kind to me and would
take time to play awhile.
    Seldom do I stop to recall things of the
past. Yet many things do I remember that now
bring a smile to my face. ———
    I am now thirteen years, six months of
age. My birthday is easy to remember, April 21, as
I was born on my mother's birthday and as my mother often says, "Easter Sunday too!" Little do I

Illustrating school work of a 5th Grader, Peggy Patrick, who
started Italic in 3rd Grade (Caledonia, N.Y.), a 9th Grader,
Larry Larocca who, after 1-1/2 weeks, wrote an entire
Ecology Report in his new hand (Greenwich, Conn.), and an
8th Grader who helped start an Italic Club when in 5th Grade,
James Herkimer (Caledonia, N.Y.)

2/2/77   Alex Atwood

Let every nation know
Whether it wishes us well or ill
That we shall pay any price
Bear any burden, meet any hardship,
Support any friend, oppose any foe
To assure the survival and success
    of Liberty.
            John F. Kennedy

Alex Atwood, 4th Grade, after 4-1/2 months
Kings Park, L.I., N.Y.

Beautiful

Beautiful faces are they that wear
The light of a pleasant spirit there;
Beautiful hands are they that do
Deeds that are noble, good and true;
Beautiful feet are they that go
Swiftly to lighten another's woe.
            McGuffey's Second Reader

Tom Norton, 10, 4th Grade, Wilton, Conn.

Beautiful

Beautiful faces are they that wear
The light of a pleasant spirit there;
Beautiful hands are they that do
Deeds that are noble, good and true;
Beautiful feet are they that go
Swiftly to lighten another's woe.
            McGuffey's Second Reader

Teresa Murphy, 11, 6th Grade
    St. John's Parish Day School, Tampa, Fla.
    Winner of 1st Prize in National Competition-
Survey-Exhibit

We hold these truths to be self evident: That all men are created equal,
    that they are endowed by their Creator with certain unalienable
    rights, that among these are Life, Liberty, and the pursuit of
    Happiness; that, to secure these rights, Governments are instituted
    among Men, deriving their just powers from the consent of the
    governed; that, whenever any form of Government, becomes
    destructive of the ends, it is the Right of the People to alter or to
    abolish it, and to institute new Government, laying its foundations
    on such principles, and organizing its powers in such form, as to
    them shall seem most likely to effect their Safety and Happiness.
        From "The Declaration of Independence" (July 4, 1776)
            Diana Blencowe, Scripsit

A 12th Grader after a few months. Greenwich, Conn.

My Easter Bonnet

I have an Easter bonnet,
It seems a little big.
I think it must be Mommie's
A funny sort of rig.

I love to try on Mommie's
It seems to be such fun.
But if she sees and catches me
I think I better run!

－Jocelyn Hilliard

scripsit-Robert McCombs

A 4th Grader, after 1 year's study of Italic in school
Caledonia, New York

The Artist and the Patron

Too often in the past, we have thought of the artist as an idler and dilettante and of the lover of arts as somehow sissy or effete. We have done both an injustice. The life of the artist is, in relation to his work, stern and lonely. He has labored hard, often amid deprivation, to perfect his skill. He has turned aside from quick success in order to strip his vision of everything secondary or cheapening. His working life is marked by intense application and intense discipline. As for the lover of arts, it is he who, by subjecting himself to the sometimes disturbing experience of art, sustains the artist — and seeks only the reward that his life will, in consequence, be the more fully lived.

From President John F. Kennedy's Introduction
to Creative America (1962)

Linda Elkins, 9th Grade winner of First Prize in
The National Handwriting Competition, 1963
Caledonia, New York

The Twenty-Third Psalm

The Lord is my shepherd; I shall n
He maketh me to lie down in gree
he leadeth me beside the still w
He restoreth my soul: he leadeth m
paths of righteousness for his n
Yea, though I walk through the val
shadow of death, I will fear no evi
with me; thy rod and thy staff t
Thou preparest a table before me in
mine enemies: thou anointest my
my cup runneth over.
Surely goodness and mercy shall fo
all the days of my life: and I w
in the house of the Lord for eve

S. Warren-Scripsit

But it was not its size that no
pressed my companions; it was the kn
edge that seven hundred thousand po
in gold lay somewhere buried below i
spreading shadows. The thought of th
money as they drew nearer, swallowed u
their previous terrors. Their eyes burne
their heads; their feet grew speedier an
lighter; their whole soul was bound up
that fortune, their whole lifetime of ex
travagance and pleasure, that lay wai
ing there for each of them.

from "Treasure Island"
by Robert Louis Steve

Keeping at it vs. Giving up

To give up a project because it looks as though you will never succeed in achieving the goal is folly, because it is impossible for you to know how close to the goal you are until you have actually completed the work. It might be the very next instant when all the work you have put into the project will suddenly come into focus and the goal will be won! Or, with a new point gained in your understanding of the work, you will suddenly find all remaining toil much easier.

Once I climbed a mountain in the High Sierras of California, whose side was terraced by nature in gigantic plateaus. Upon reaching a plateau after each gruelling climb, it appeared that the next one would be the top. This continued on and on. I could have given up at any stage, not knowing how close I was—or how far—from the top. Persevering, I finally reached the summit and was rewarded by a grand view of lakes and plains, shared only by my companion and a woodchuck. The reward was well worth the persistence in rejecting all temptations to give up. Fred Eager

S. Warren-Scripsit

A 12th Grader illustrates The Calligraphic Mode, A Compromise, and The Cursive Mode of Italic Handwriting
Greenwich, Conn.

82

Slant your pen so that the edge of your pen is in line with the edge of the pen in the drawings. For right-handed writers the entire pen will align with the drawings. For left-handed writers using the left oblique pens, the EDGE of the pen should align with the edge of the pen in the drawings.

Now make pluses. If your pen is slanted correctly, the two strokes will be equal in thickness. DO NOT TURN YOUR PEN BETWEEN STROKES!

Now make boxes. If your pen is slanted correctly, the sides of the boxes will be of equal thickness.

Now hold your pen in TOO FLAT a position. Pluses and boxes will look like this:

Now hold your pen in TOO STEEP a position. Pluses and boxes will look like this:

Now once more hold your pen in a correct, slanted position and write the alphabet with pluses between each letter. KEEP THE PEN SLANTED as you cross the page!

+a +a +b +b +c +c +d
+d +e +e +f +f +g +g
+h +h +i +j +k +k +l +
+m +m +n +n +o +o
+p +p +q +q +r +r +s +
+s +t +t +u +u +v +v
+w +w +x +y +z +z

Until your teacher says that you have mastered pen-angle, practice letters and words
always with a + or ☐ between them. If a plus or a box looks like this: + ☐
or like this: + ☐   DO NOT write the letter or word until you have turned
your pen so that your plus or box looks like this: + ☐ + ☐ +   Then KEEP
your pen slanted as you write the letter or word. Work hard at this and be
patient with yourself and you will master it sooner than you think.

1. Practice these letters and watch the slant at the tops of the letters.

+b +b +d +d +h +h +k +l

2. Practice these letters and watch the slant at the bottoms of your strokes.

+h +m +m +n +n +m +

3. Practice these letters and keep the two strokes equal in thickness.

+t +t +f +f +t +t +f +f

4a. Practice these letters and keep the serifs thin.

+i +i +u +u +n +n +m

+m +a +a +d +d +i +n

4b. Practice these words and be certain that your pen is slanted so that you get
the thin strokes in the right places of the letters as in the models.

+an   +am   +man   +it

+aim   +ant   +and   +is

+aunt   +ear   +end   +me

+men   +need   +dip   +in

+nip   +miss   +under   +

+until   +hunt   +hum

+hammer   +melon   +

+mastery +   +multiply

84

Trace each word and write it over and over across the entire line with ✛ or ☐ between
to check your pen angle.

✛ across ✛ across ✛ across ✛ across ✛ across ✛ across ✛

☐ arithmetic ☐ arithmetic ☐

✛ August

☐ bicycle

✛ bought

☐ caught

✛ climbed

☐ cushion

✛ December

☐ different

✛ friends

☐ gather

✛ Halloween

☐ health

✛ highest

☐ January

✛ laughed

☐ meadow

✛ minutes

☐ November

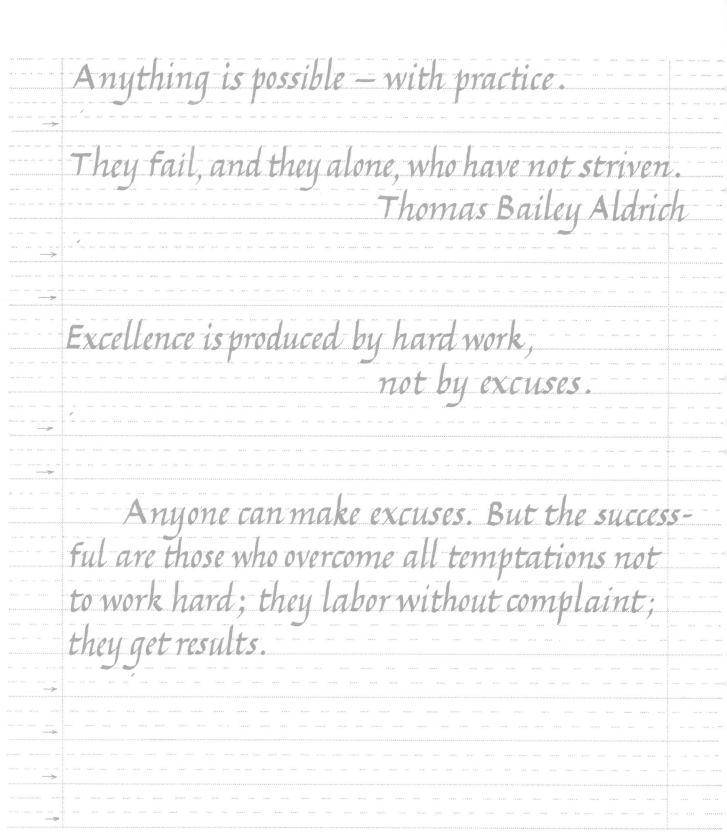

Anything is possible — with practice.

They fail, and they alone, who have not striven.
— Thomas Bailey Aldrich

Excellence is produced by hard work,
not by excuses.

Anyone can make excuses. But the successful are those who overcome all temptations not to work hard; they labor without complaint; they get results.

Now work through the book again with your broad edged pen, starting at page 30. Whenever you come to a poem, instead of that poem, use one on the following pages which has been keyed to come after the page you have worked on.

There was an old owl who lived in an oak;
The more he heard the less he spoke.
The less he spoke, the more he heard.
Why aren't we like that wise old bird!

See a pin and pick it up,
All the day you'll have good luck.
See a pin and let it lie,
You'll be sorry by and by.

Now pages 35, 37, 38

A Centipede

A centipede was happy quite,
    Until a frog in fun
Said, "Pray, which leg comes after which?"
This raised her mind to such a pitch,
She lay distracted in a ditch
    Considering how to run.

                    Author Unknown

A Beginning of Adventures

From far-away lands the south wind blew,
And brought me a tale that is strange and new;
A tale full of spices and music and flowers,
And many adventures to fill the hours,
And quaint, happy people who live there too—
And

now
    I am telling the tale to you!

            from NADITA by Grace Moon

Now pages 39, 46–48

Hold Fast Your Dreams

Hold fast your dreams!
Within your heart
Keep one still, secret spot
Where dreams may go,
And sheltered so,
May thrive and grow—
Where doubt and fear are not.
Oh, keep a place apart
Within your heart,
For little dreams to go.

Louise Driscoll

When you're perfect
people can't wait
to pick you apart.
Paramount Chicken

The Wind
The wind whispered a secret to me,
That only an artist would know.
A beautiful blanket of green,
Lay beneath the snow.
                    Margaret Manley

Snow
Snow makes things white where it falls.
The bushes look like cotton balls.
And places where I always play,
Look like somewhere else today.
                    Richard De Cost

The Optimist
The optimist fell twelve stories
And at each window bar,
He shouted to his friends,
"All right so far..."
                    Cathy Rayhill

These poems are
from a Fifth Grade's
Newspaper,
Grand Island, New York.

Now pages 52-54

Work while you work
    Play while you play;
One thing each time,
    That is the way.

    All that you do,
        Do with your might;
    Things done by halves
        Are not done right.

            McGuffey's Primer

Now pages 56, 59

The Owl and the Pussycat

The Owl and the Pussycat went to sea
In a beautiful pea-green boat;
They took some honey and plenty of money
Wrapped up in a five pound note.
The owl looked up to the stars above,
And sang to a small guitar,
"Oh lovely Pussy, O Pussy, my love,
What a beautiful Pussy you are
You are,
You are!
What a beautiful Pussy you are!"

an excerpt   Edward Lear

Now page 62

O magnify the Lord with me,
  and let us exalt his name together.
I sought the Lord, and he heard me,
  and delivered me from all my fears...
The angel of the Lord
  encampeth round about
    them that fear him,
    and delivereth them.
        Psalms 34:3-7

        Millstone or Milestone
A millstone or a milestone,
Which shall it be?
Shall I hang it heavy around my neck
And drag it along with me,
Or stand it up by the roadside
To mark one more victory?
        Peter J. Henniker-Heaton

Now pages 63–66

Gerard, the Giraffe

Our friend Gerard is a young giraffe
The pinkish tan of a Jersey calf,
With sharp brown ears and soft brown eyes
And a neck that can wear 16 bow ties.

He chews up derbies and silk cravats,
The veils and flowers off ladies' hats,
And the bright gold eagles on flagpole tops,
For Gerard declares, as he licks his chops,
That there's nothing a young giraffe enjoys
Like EATING!
In fact, they're a lot like BOYS!

Ethel Jacobson

Now pages 68, 70, 73

America the Beautiful

O beautiful for spacious skies,
For amber waves of grain,
For purple mountain majesties
Above the fruited plain!

America, America!
God shed his grace on thee,
And crown thy good with brotherhood
From sea to shining sea!

Katherine Lee Bates

Copy this poem 3 or 4 times or more until it is the very best you can do. When you start
it each time, keep on until the end. Do not throw it away after one or two lines.
After each completion, stop, look, and decide what you can do to improve it the next time.

Now it is time to write smaller, in preparation for using the medium edged pen.

Notice that with only two guide lines, the main part of your writing, the "x-height" is between these lines. Now it is important to find the half-way point in the large spaces between lines for your ascenders and descenders. The size of capitals is midway between the x-height and the ascender height.

a c e i m n o r s u v w x z b d h k l g j p q y F A B C D

aa a bb b cc c dd d ee e ff f gg g
hh h ii i jj j kk k ll l mm m m
nn n oo o pp p qq q rr r ss s tt t
uu u vv v ww w xx x yy y zz z
AA A BB B CC C DD D EE E FF F
GG G HH H II I JJ J KK K LL L
MM M NN N OO O PP P
QQ Q RR R SS S TT T UU U
VV V WW W XX X YY Y
ZZ Z 1 2 3 4 5 6 7 8 9 0

A quick brown fox jumps over the lazy dog.
Copy:
Copy:
Seven men mentioned many machines that ran.
Copy:

oranges oranges oranges oranges oranges oranges oranges

October

peanuts

queen

quiet

remembered

riddle

September

squeeze

surprises

swimming

Thanksgiving

thumb

Thursday

tumble

upstairs

valentine

watermelon

yesterday

believe

adventures

avenue

bandage

catsup

chocolate

Trace and copy No. 1. Then simply copy No. 2. See if your copying-only is as good as your trace-and-copy. Then trace-and-copy No. 3, copy No. 4, and so on, tracing-and-copying the odd numbered quotations, and copying-only the even numbered ones.

1. Nothing is impossible to a willing heart. – John H. Page

2.   Happiness cannot come from without.
        It must come from within.
                Helen Keller

3. Better slip with foot than by tongue – Benjamin Franklin

4. Joys are our wings, sorrows are our spurs – Richter

5. Give what you have; to some it may be
             better than you dare to think.
                Longfellow

6. What you dislike in another,
          take care to correct in yourself.
             Thomas Spratt

REVIEW OF PEN ANGLE with MEDIUM PEN

Keep your pen slanted so that the edge of your pen lines up with the little lines (dots) you see next to the models:

Now make pluses. If your pen is slanted correctly, the two strokes will be equal in thickness. DO NOT TURN YOUR PEN BETWEEN STROKES!

Now make boxes. If your pen is slanted correctly, the sides of the boxes will be of equal thickness.

Now hold your pen in TOO FLAT a position. Pluses and boxes will look like this:

Now hold your pen in TOO STEEP a position. Pluses and boxes will look like this:

Now once more hold your pen in a correct, slanted position.

Now write the alphabet with pluses between each letter. KEEP THE PEN SLANTED.

+a +a +b +b +c +c +d +d
+e +e +f +f +g +g +h +h +i +i
+j +j +k +k +l +l +m +m
+n +n +o +o +p +p +q +q
+r +r +s +s +t +t +u +u
+v +v +w +w +x +x +y
+y +z +z +a +b +c +d +e

TO SEE IF YOUR PEN IS CORRECTLY SLANTED:
1. Look carefully at the <u>tops</u> of these letters for a slant: b d h k l NOT l or l
2. Look carefully at the <u>bottoms</u> of these letters for a slant: h m n NOT m or n
3. See if both strokes of f and t are equally thick: f t NOT f t or f t
4. See if your serifs and joining strokes stay thin: m man NOT man
5. See if your writing is of even thickness on both sides of the page.

+crumble crumble crumble+ + crumble+

+dangerous+

+doughnut+

+dwarf+

+envelope+

+favorite+

+February+

+furniture+

+geography

+grammar

+laughing

+library

+listening

+machine

+measure

+mountains

+multiplication

+neighbors

+old-fashioned

+pasture

+practice

+questions

+rough

+surprised

+treasure

Trace and copy No. 1. Then simply copy No. 2. See if your copying-only is as good as your trace-and-copy. Then trace-and-copy No. 3, copy No. 4, and so on, tracing-and-copying the odd numbered quotations, and copying-only the even numbered ones.

1. Face the situation fearlessly,

2.   and soon there will be no situation to face.   Anon

3. All that stands between most men,

4.   and the top of the ladder is the ladder.   Anon

5. In character, in manners, in style, in all things,

6.   the supreme excellence is simplicity.   Longfellow

7. When love and skill work together,

8.   expect a masterpiece.   Ruskin

9. Never say, "Can't!" Say, "Not yet,—but SOON,

10.   with practice."   Eager

The Park

I'm glad that I
Live near a park

For in the winter
After dark

The park lights shine
As bright and still

As dandelions
On a hill.

James S. Tippet

Write this short poem four times, or more, until it is the very best you can do.
When you start it each time, keep on until the end. Do not throw it away after
one or two lines. After each completion, stop, look, and decide what you can
do to improve it the next time.

Psalm 100

Make a joyful noise unto the Lord, all ye lands.
Serve the Lord with gladness:
Come before His presence with singing.

Know ye that the Lord He is God:
It is He that hath made us, and not we ourselves;
We are His people, and the sheep of His pasture.

Enter into His gates with thanksgiving,
And into His courts with praise:
Be thankful unto Him, and bless His name.

For the Lord is good;
His mercy is everlasting;
And His truth endureth to all generations.

ADVICE TO WRITERS
FOR THE DAILY PRESS

When you've got a thing to say,
Say it! Don't take half a day.
When your tale's got little in it,
Crowd the whole thing in a minute!
Life is short - a fleeting vapor -
Don't you fill the whole blamed paper
With a tale which, at a pinch,
Could be cornered in an inch!
Boil her down until she simmers,
Polish her until she glimmers.

                    Joel Chandler Harris

WEEKLY ALPHABET AND DAILY WARM-UP

Daily work on this Weekly Alphabet and Warm-up will build a beautiful, flowing Italic into your hand. Practice it faithfully EVERY DAY from now on. Use the Daily Warm-Up Guide Sheet for your practice. Work with patience and see your writing improve day after day, week after week.

For the idea of the daily warm-up I am indebted to Professor Lloyd J. Reynolds of Reed College, Portland, Oregon. To his warm-up I have simply added the weekly alphabet idea.

1. WEEKLY ALPHABET: Every day write five letters of the alphabet, each letter three times, underlining the one you think is best. Do this with the minuscule (small letter) alphabet one week, next week with the capitals. On the following weeks alternate between the two alphabets.

2. ARCADE. Keep high-branching, full, elliptical arches. Write a check (✔) above any places where you branch too low or have pointed instead of elliptical arches.

3. m's JOINED. Arches separated by single lower curves.

4. mumu—contrary movements.

5. One line each of two words. Use different words each day from page 106.

6. Special extra practice on faults. Here is a place to practice the letter shapes which you have trouble with, or an opportunity to work especially for even alignment (overlapping the guide lines slightly), or for more even slant or spacing.

As you write across the lines in the warm-up, start slowly and gradually add speed, except on the Weekly Alphabet, which should always be written slowly with your very best shapes.

On Items 2 to 5, place checks above any of your branching letters (m, n, h, k, r) which branch too low, then slow down. Write no faster than the fastest speed at which you can keep the branching high with elliptical arches.

First Day   Date: _____

1 _aaabbbcccdddeee_____
2 _mm mm mm mm m m_____
3 _mmm mmm mmm✔_____
4 _mumu mumu mumu_____
5 _hum hum hum hum_____
  _acme acme acme acme_____
6 _m am am llbll bb m m m dd_____

Second Day   Date: _____

1 _fff ggg hhh iii jjj_____
2 _mm mm mm mm mm mm mm_____
3 _mmm mmm mmm mmm_____
4 _mumu mumu mumu_____
5 _many many many many_____
  _dip dip dip dip dip dip dip_____
6 _m llll billabong m billabong_____

aaabbbcccdddeee‖fff ggghhhiiijjj‖ kkklllmmmnnnooo‖
pppqqqrrrssstttt‖ uuuvvvwwwxxxyyyzzz
AAA BBB CCC DDD EEE‖FFFGGGHHHIIIJJJ‖
KKK LLL MMM NNN OOO‖PPPQQQRRRSSSTTT
UUU VVV WWW XXX YYY ZZZ‖ 1 2 3 4 5 6 7 8 9 10

ha any name angry homing command maintain as ham
anna mouse amount numeral dominion hi ant mime
amuse nation amiable humanity ad man aunt manor
common honor announce my aim hail minute avocado
monogram minuet ay mat ahem hence accent ivy ice
until unite mine mum hats liar under nice joins aha ahem
maul cat dog dam ate night day ammunition cannon
pistol mat cold cotton control common commerce cook
occupy occasion ocean enemy alone complete done enter hour
monkey poem neighbor nothing number moment meaning
murmur honest honey hundred handsome kingdom kindly
render remark remain armor cannon danger enemy dig
human den ditch done lawn lamb lay limit little aunt
man announce accident monster automobile nip admit
active nut none accept account never command use ugly
come camp unity intend include into meander memo
handle commune nominate at hag dear mummy banana
humming behemoth ho den hair under murmur ancient
monument do nut doughnut hamburger hot dog katsup
cone sundae milkshake acacia nominal dominoes mud
meander manger adamant nuisance amen undone
meaning imitation him arm dragon hunting hiking
tenting swimming skiing meter cross country backpack
mountain foothill knoll trail wooded underbrush fire
kindling matches flint knapsack sleeping bag fishing

Tricks to help you get strong flourished capitals.

B Keep it flat on top and bottom, and keep the middle horizontal.

E F To get the serifs on the ends of the two upper arms: when you finish the stroke, twist your pen onto its left corner and lift off the paper in a downward movement.

T Don't let the cross stroke slant or curve except at its right or left ends.

B D P R When your top stroke crosses the vertical stem in these letters, you must be moving the pen either horizontally across, or diagonally down. If you are moving upward, they will appear weak. Strong: **B B P P D R R R** Weak: **B R D P**

Trace one letter (like one A), copy it, then write several on your own paper, then another letter, and more on your own paper, to get the most out of this page.

A A A A A A A A A A A B B B B B B B

C C C C C D D D D D D E E E E E F F F

G G G G G H H H H H H I I I I I I II II

JJ J J JJ J J J J J KK K K K K K K LL L L

M M M M M M M M M M M M M M

N N N N N N N O O O P P P P P Q Q

Q Q R R R R S S S T T T T T

U U U VV V V V V W W W XX X X

Y Y Y Y Y Y Y Y Y Y ZZ Z Z Z Z

& & & & & & & & e e e e e

Alaska   British Columbia

Denver   Europe   Florida   Go

Hawaii   Idaho   New Jersey

Kentucky   Louisiana   Maine

       Nebraska   Ohio   Pennsylvania

          Quebec   Rome   Seattle

     Toronto   Utah   Vermont

Washington   Xerxes   Yukon

Zanzibar   1 2 3 4 5 6 7 8 99

f f f f g g gg p p p q q x x y y z z

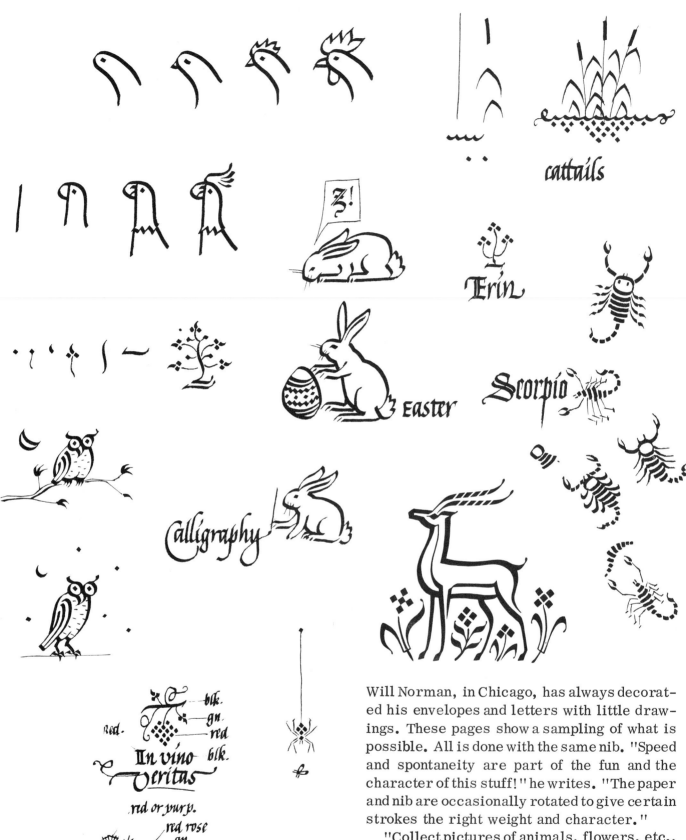

cattails

Z!

Erin

Easter

Scorpio

Calligraphy

Will Norman, in Chicago, has always decorated his envelopes and letters with little drawings. These pages show a sampling of what is possible. All is done with the same nib. "Speed and spontaneity are part of the fun and the character of this stuff!" he writes. "The paper and nib are occasionally rotated to give certain strokes the right weight and character."

"Collect pictures of animals, flowers, etc., and try to capture the simple essence of them in as few lines as possible. Stick with one design for a long time and each repetition should eliminate some imperfection until a simple but lively abstraction says 'Rose' or 'Spider'."

De furore Normannorum
Libera nos Domine

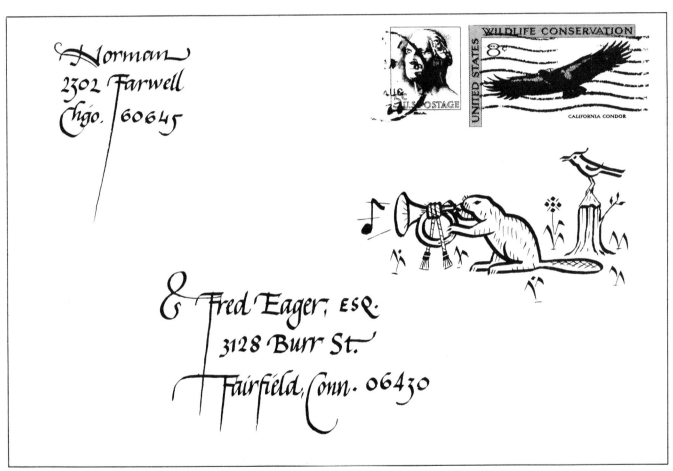

Norman
2302 Farwell
Chgo. 60645

WILDLIFE CONSERVATION
UNITED STATES
U.S. POSTAGE
CALIFORNIA CONDOR

& Fred Eager, ESQ.
3128 Burr St.
Fairfield, Conn. 06430

Regards,
Will

Geography

Islands and peninsulas, continents and capes,
Dromedaries, cassowaries, elephants and apes,
Rivers, lakes and waterfalls, whirlpools and the sea,
Valley-beds and mountain-tops — are all Geography!

The capitals of Europe with so many curious names,
The North Pole and the South Pole and Vesuvius in flames,
Rice-fields, ice-fields, cotton-fields, fields of maize and tea,
The Equator and the Hemispheres — are all Geography!

The very streets I live in, and the meadows where I play,
Are just as much Geography as countries far away,
Where yellow girls and coffee boys are learning about _me_,
The little white-skinned stranger who is in Geography!

Eleanor Farjeon

TO BUILD SPEED

To transform your slow careful Italic into a free, rapid handwriting will take some special practice. Here are steps to take.

RHYTHMIC WRITING

1. Daily warm-up: Keep branching high on m, n, h.

2. Write words over and over. One line, at least, for each word. Find the rhythm of each word and enjoy it. Use words from pages 32, 43-85, or 97-112.

3. Take a short quotation, one of your favorite, or one from pages, 34, 51, 86, 98, or 101. Write it three or four times rhythmically.

4. Do the above steps with AND WITHOUT the edged pen.

DEVELOPING SPEED.

CAUTION: Never write so fast that m's, n's, and h's don't branch high. Then your writing will always be readable.

1. Write one letter over and over, gradually increasing speed.

2. Write a word over and over, gradually increasing speed. Use words from pages listed in No. 2 above.

3. Write a short quotation or alphabet sentence over and over, gradually increasing speed (See No. 3 above). Write for two minutes. Count the letters, divide by 2. That is your speed in letters per minute (LPM).

4. Copy a passage for 10 minutes. Count the words, divide by 10 and that is your speed in LPM.

5. Have someone dictate to you at different speeds.

6. Take notes.

MAIN GOALS IN RAPID HANDWRITING:

Readability: Keep branching high!

Speed: Build it gradually—don't be too finicky about beauty here. Readability is the main thing to be concerned about.

HELPS: ALWAYS:

—Watch branching: Keep it high and arching, not spikey:

Many men are mending the

NOT

Many men are mending the

—Practice with and without the edged pen.

—Continually repeat all exercises above.

—It will help you to fulfill the goals of readability and speed if you will write smaller and open your spacing up wider. (See Introducing the Two Modes of Italic Handwriting on page 113.)

—Make ascenders and descenders shorter and join to them when writing fast.

finally there are the tall silhouettes of tall buildings filled with silly people wearing habitual fake smiles.

—Always use the simpler letter shapes with speed.

—Always intersperse your speed practice with slow, careful practice. It will be enjoyable and will help with your control as you build speed.

The average adult handwriting speed is about 100 LPM. A student who will be going to college, taking notes, etc., should work to build his writing to between 100 and 140 LPM during the last years of high school. Then taking notes will not "ruin" his handwriting.

I have always found that I can write fast enough including note-taking with a free-flowing edged pen. But you need an ink that will not gum. Quink or Pelikan 4001 are fine for speed. For slow work you can use the heavier Stephen's Calligraph Ink, Artone Fountain Pen India, Pelikan Fountain Pen India, etc. (For dip pens, Higgins Engrossing is a good ink to use.)

advertisement
appreciated
banquet
carriage
earthquake
especially
handkerchief
hygiene
knowledge
librarian
neighborhood
orchestra
paragraph
physical
catalogue
considerable
delicious
scandalous
discipline
equipped
knuckle
vanilla
volunteer
abbreviation
alphabetically

THE CALLIGRAPHIC MODE

Here is the alphabet written with the medium pen using the No. 1 Guide Sheet (5/32"). The spacing between verticals is about half the height of x, and they are packed closely together so that the spacing is very even. The spacing is by eye and no joins are used. This is beautiful but not quite as easy to read. These tall, narrow shapes should never be written quickly or be used for handwriting for they become spikey with speed and make a hand difficult to read. But for slow, careful work, the beauty of this Calligraphic Mode can't be beat.

Alternate shapes are given. No. 1 shapes are fine with the Calligraphic Mode or for rapid handwriting, but No. 2 shapes should be used ONLY when doing slow work with the Calligraphic Mode. If used in handwriting they will become a hard-to-break habit, and will wreck the slant of a rapid hand.

aa a a bb b b cc c c dd d d ee e e ff f f f
gg g g hh h h ü i j j kk k k ll mm m m
m nn n n oo o o pp p p qq q q rr ss s s s
l + - = tt t t u uu u u vv v v ww w w xx x x
yy y y zz z z "b b bdd d hh h kk k ll l l
"g gg g g qee e e yyy y y "b b d h k l

THE CURSIVE MODE of Italic Handwriting: Now here is the Cursive Mode of Italic Handwriting. The medium pen is still used, but the letters are much stumpier, short, and all vertical strokes are spaced farther apart.

This is the type of Italic we recommend for really fast handwriting, and for a person's personal rapid hand. In this mode you can write faster, but because of the open spacing, it is still easy to read. Use Guide Sheet No. 4.

aa a a a bb b b c c c d d d ce e e f f f g g g
h h h i i j j k k k l l m m m n n n o o o o
p p p q q q r r r s s s tt t t u u u v v v w w
w x x x y y y z z z "b b b d d h h k k l l
yy y y g g g g 1 1 2 2 3 4 4 5 5 6 6 7 7
8 8 8 9 9 9 . This hand can also be quite lovely when
written slowly. Spacing in this Cursive Mode is by the rhythm
of the joins with the pen held constantly at the 45° angle.

ALPHABET SENTENCES

These alphabet sentences are useful for developing rhythm and speed. They illustrate the two modes of Italic Handwriting. The Cursive Mode is shown written at different speeds.

A quick brown fox jumps over the lazy dog. (33 letters)

Picking just six quinces, new farm hand proves strong but lazy. (51)

For civilization, Marxist thought just must be quickly replaced by ways of freedom. (69)

The vixen jumped quickly on her foe, barking with zeal. (44)

As we explored the gulf in Zanzibar, we quickly moved closer to the jutting rocks. (66)

Joe was pleased with our gift of quail, mink, zebra, and clever oryx. (53)

Travelling beneath the azure sky in our jolly ox-cart, we often hit bumps quite hard. (68)

Alfredo just must bring very exciting news to the plaza quickly. (53)

If I give you cloth with quartz beads: onyx, jasper, amethyst, keep it. (54)

Anxious Al waved back his pa from the zinc quarry just sighted. (51)

Venerable Will played jazz sax 'til 3 o'clock in the morning before he quit. (60)

Back home after swing so, he expired with quizzicality. (46)

Adjusting quiver and bow, Zompyc killed the fox. (39)

A foxy, quick, clever cat in Switzerland was hit by a fancy sports job with bumpy seats and a grumpy driver. (85)

COMPROMISE BETWEEN THE TWO MODES

The writing you have learned in this book is a compromise about half-way between these two modes. This compromise hand is very useful for one's personal handwriting, although it is not quite as beautiful as the Calligraphic Mode (for special uses, quotations, etc.), nor can it be written quite as rapidly as the Cursive Mode, which is more practical for note-taking.

As a Little Child

Think about holiness,
Open your thought to it.
It is the essence of all that you are.
Think about godliness,
Hold it quite close to you;
It is the substance that lights every star.
Think about tenderness,
Cherish its Christly touch.

If with these qualities you would be blessed
Think about willingness,
Make it the all of you—
It is the key to God's kingdom expressed.

Mildred L. Hocker

Now

If you have hard work to do,
    Do it now.
Today the skies are clear and blue,
Tomorrow clouds may come in view,
Yesterday is not for you;
    Do it now.

        If you have a song to sing,
            Sing it now.
        Let the notes of gladness ring
        Clear as song of bird in Spring,
        Let every day some music bring;
            Sing it now.

If you have kind words to say,
    Say them now.
Tomorrow may not come your way,
Do a kindness while you may,
Loved ones will not always stay;
    Say them now.

        If you have a smile to show,
            Show it now.
        Make hearts happy, roses grow,
        Let the friends around you know
        The love you have before they go;
            Show it now.
                    Charles R. Skinner

For more advanced work, for fuller treatment of flourishes, the calligraphic mode, the cursive mode for rapid personal handwriting, speed work, work with fine pen, etc., you will enjoy The Italic Way to Beautiful Handwriting by the author of this book.

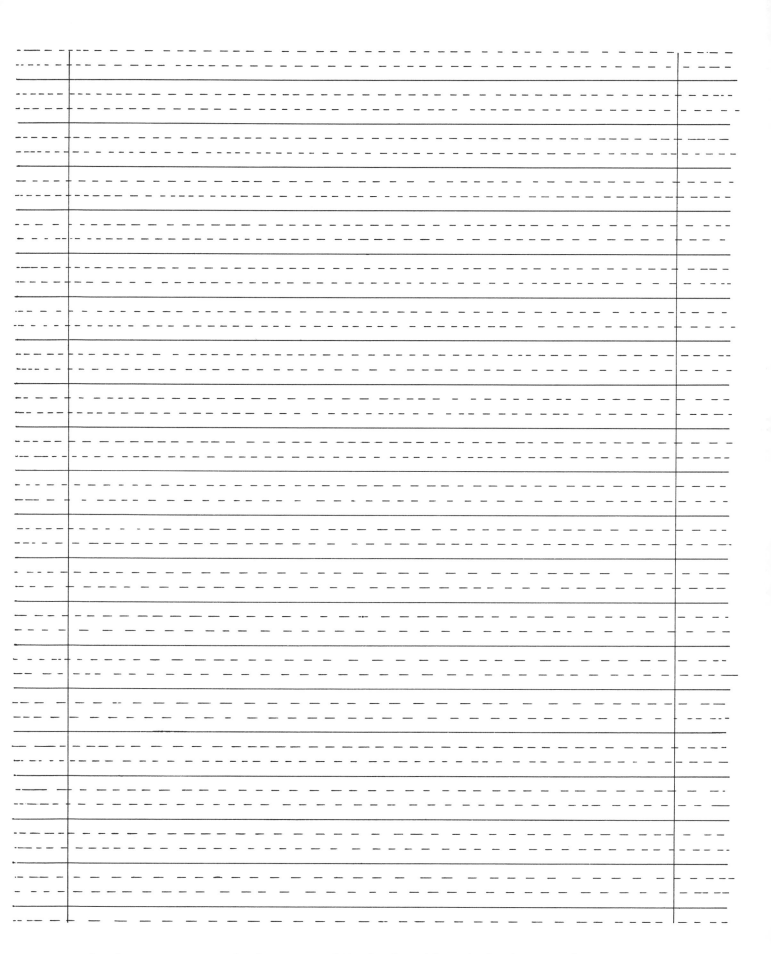

Guide Sheet No. 1: For the first part of the book and broad edged pen work.
Also for Medium Pen in the Calligraphic Mode (page 113)

Guide Sheet No. 1: For the first part of the book and broad edged pen work.
Also for Medium Pen in the Calligraphic Mode (page 113)

Guide Sheet No. 2: Medium Pen. For all medium pen work before page 113

Guide Sheet No. 2: Medium Pen. For all medium pen work before page 113

Daily Warm-up of _____

NAME

First Day   Date: _____

1 _____
2 _____
3 _____
4 _____
5 _____
  _____
6 _____
  _____
  _____

Second Day   Date: _____

1 _____
2 _____
3 _____
4 _____
5 _____
  _____
6 _____
  _____
  _____

Third Day   Date: _____

1 _____
2 _____
3 _____

Third Day, continued

4 _____
5 _____
  _____
6 _____
  _____

Fourth Day   Date: _____

1 _____
2 _____
3 _____
4 _____
5 _____
  _____
6 _____
  _____

Fifth Day   Date: _____

1 _____
2 _____
3 _____
4 _____
5 _____
  _____
6 _____
  _____

Guide Sheet No. 3: Warm-up Guide Sheet

Daily Warm-up of _____

First Day Date: _____

1 _____
2 _____
3 _____
4 _____
5 _____
  _____
6 _____
  _____

Second Day Date: _____

1 _____
2 _____
3 _____
4 _____
5 _____
  _____
6 _____
  _____

Third Day Date: _____

1 _____
2 _____
3 _____

Third Day, continued

4 _____
5 _____
  _____
6 _____
  _____

Fourth Day Date: _____

1 _____
2 _____
3 _____
4 _____
5 _____
  _____
6 _____
  _____

Fifth Day Date: _____

1 _____
2 _____
3 _____
4 _____
5 _____
  _____
6 _____
  _____

Guide Sheet No. 3: Warm-up Guide Sheet

Guide Sheet No. 4: Medium Pen: Cursive Mode (after page 113)

Guide Sheet No. 4: Medium Pen: Cursive Mode (after page 113)

NAME

Other Comments

II

Marking: Excellent = +, Average = blank, Needs extra work = ✓
Grading: No faults = A+, 1 fault = A, 2 = B+, 3 = B, 4 = C, 5 = D, 6 = E, 7 = F

Neat Papers
Carefulness
Spacing
Joins
Serifs
Alignment (size)
Slant
Capitals
v, w, x, y, z
f, t, s
b, p
m, n, h, r
o, c, e
a, d, g, u
Pen Angle

I

Marking: 1 (no. of pages); o (this item missing)
Grading: No item missing = A, 1 missing - B
2 - C, 3 - D, 4 - E, 5 - F.

Self-grading of one page
Speed Work (after page 64)
No. pages of School Work
No. of Poems
No. pages of Assigned Work
Extra Practice on Faults
Daily Warm-up
Weekly Alphabet

Each line is for one week. Final grade is average of I & II

GRADE		DATE
I	II	

	NAME																																
	Other Comments																																	

II — Marking: Excellent = +, Average = blank, Needs extra work = √
Grading: No faults = A+, 1 fault = A, 2 = B+, 3 = B, 4 = C, 5 = D, 6 = E, 7 = F

- Neat Papers
- Carefulness
- Spacing
- Joins
- Serifs
- Alignment (Size)
- Slant
- Capitals
- v, w, x, y, z
- f, t, s
- b, p
- m, n, h, r
- o, c, e
- a, d, g, q, u
- Pen Angle

I — Marking: 1 (no. of pages); o (this item missing)
Grading: No item missing = A. 1 missing-B
2 - C. 3 - D. 4 - E. 5 - F.

- Self-grading of one page
- Speed Work (after page 64)
- No. pages of School Work
- No. of Poems
- No. pages of Assigned Work
- Extra Practice on Faults
- Daily Warm-up
- Weekly Alphabet

Each line is for one week. Final grade is average of I & II

	GRADE I	GRADE II	DATE																														

Alphabets in this Book

abcdefghijklmno

pqrstuvwxyz

Pencil or nylon-tipped pen

abcdefghijklmnopqrstuvwxyz
ABCDEFGHIJKLMNOPQRSTUV
WXYZ 1234567890

Broad Italic Edged Pen:

abcdefghijklmnopqrstuvwxyz
ABCDEFGHIJKLMNOPQRSTUV
WXYZ 1234567890

Medium Italic Edged Pen

abcdefghijklmnopqrstuvwxyz
ABCDEFGGHIJKKLMNOPQR
STUVWXYZ 12345678910
bdhklgyohbdklz

Alphabets in this Book

abcdefghijklmno

pqrstuvwxyz

Pencil or nylon-tipped pen

abcdefghijklmnopqrstuvwxyz
ABCDEFGHIJKLMNOPQRSTUV
WXYZ 1234567890

Broad Italic Edged Pen :

abcdefghijklmnopqrstuvwxyz
ABCDEFGHIJKLMNOPQRSTUV
WXYZ 1234567890

Medium Italic Edged Pen

abcdefghijklmnopqrstuvwxyz
ABCDEFGGHIJKKLMNOPQR
STUVWXYZ 12345678910
bdhklgyohbdklz